Three Sisters

Back to the Beginning

Food is love,

3 greek sisters,

Betty, [signature], Samantha

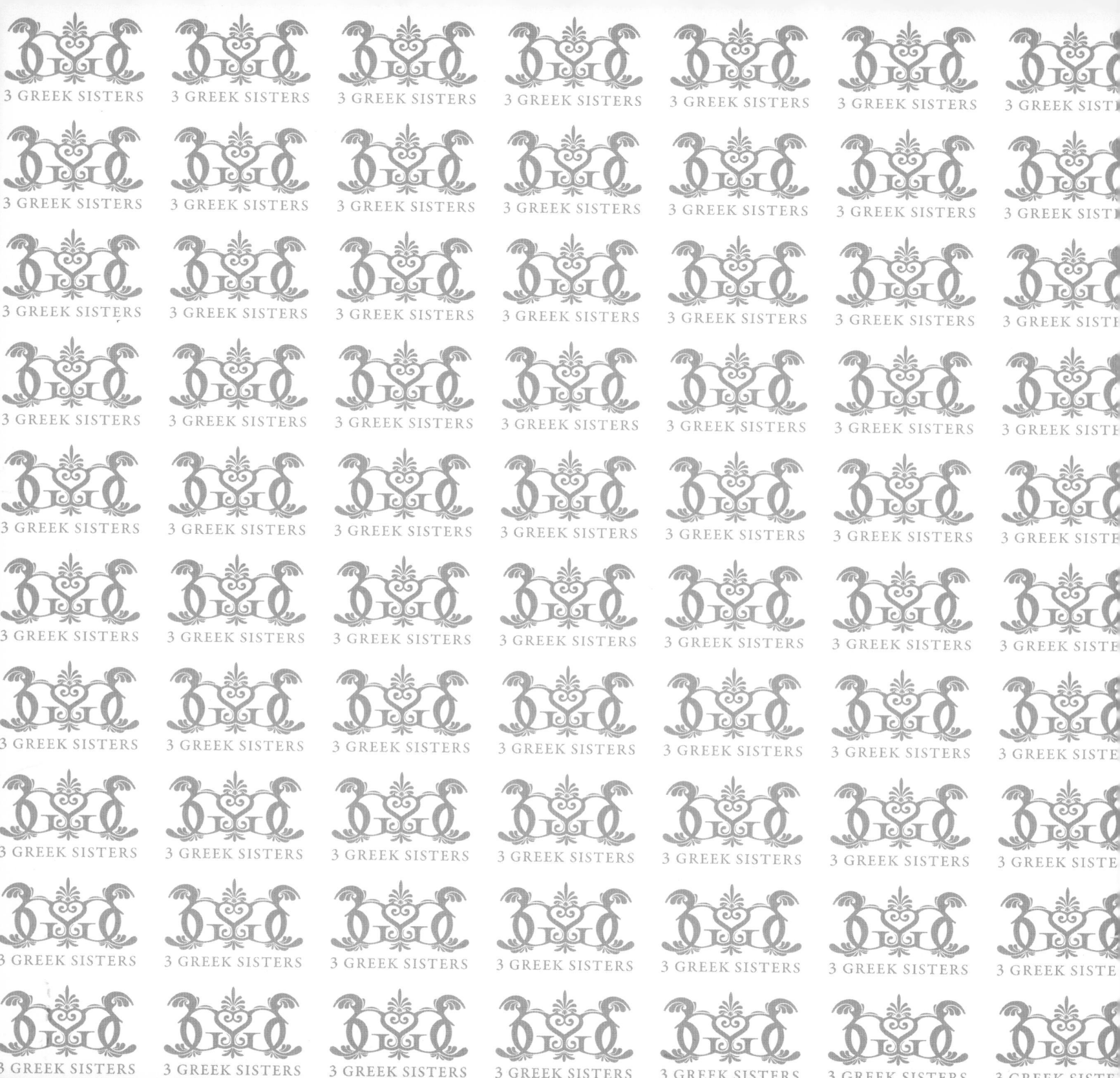

The House
Early 1900s-2011

Departure Day - Dimitri & Lefteri

Three Sisters

Back to the Beginning

Timeless Greek Recipes Made Simple

a cookbook by

Betty, Eleni & Samantha Bakopoulos

adelfes

Also by Betty, Eleni & Samantha Bakopoulos
Award-Winning & Bestselling Cookboook, *Three Sisters Around the Greek Table.*

Text & Photographs Copyright © 2013 by Betty, Eleni & Samantha Bakopoulos
Photography by Eleni Bakopoulos
Graphics by Samantha Bakopoulos

Adelfes Publishing
www.3greeksisters.com

FIRST EDITION 2013

A Catalog record for this book is available from the LIbrary of Congress
ISBN 9780981340517

PRINTED BY AMP GESTIONS IMPRESSIONS

PRINTED & BOUND IN CANADA

Departure Day - Emilia

Departure Day - Konstantina & Georgios

To anyone who has had to leave
the land of their birth
in search of a better future -
may you never forget your beginning.

To Greece.

Contents

Betty

Eleni

Samantha

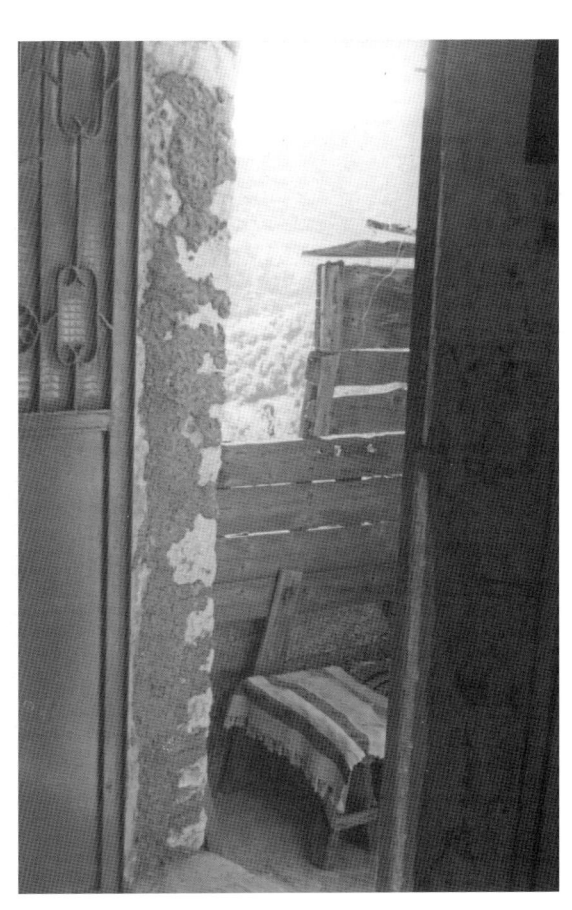

The House

In the summer of 2012, we made the decision to restore the old stone home in which our father's family had lived. It is the home our father left from as a young groom on horseback, to pick up his bride from the neighbouring village. It is the home he brought her to on their wedding night. It is the home we came to as young girls and left wiser and richer.

We couldn't help but change when we understood the extent of sadness that was required to bring about our good fortune. Our grandparents had to say goodbye to most of their children when they reached young adulthood. Since the farming life they had raised them in offered little hope for a secure future, one by one, their children left for the United States, Australia or Canada. And one by one, as the years went by, they sent the grandchildren back to meet Yiayia and Pappou, unable to stop working and visit themselves.

Come summer's end, we watched an otherwise stoic man, our grandfather, weeping on the back step of his home, unable to stand or speak to say goodbye. Each visit held for him the childlike and innocent hope that one of us would decide to stay behind. But depart we always did, having glimpsed another world, another time; having known mountain air, the Aegean Sea, the sound of a thousand crickets in an olive grove, the free and timeless pleasure of crab-hunting in the river, and the love of family.

The summer of 2012 will be remembered in our family as the summer we went back to the beginning of it all. We laid stone, we pushed dirt, we built up what had fallen, and we honoured where we came from. Our ancestral home had never been so full: full of memories, emotion, and hopes for the future. The cover of our cookbook marks a significant moment in our lives; the moment when our children walked through the gate of our grandparents' home, now our parents' home, with our mother and father, marking a new beginning for a new generation.

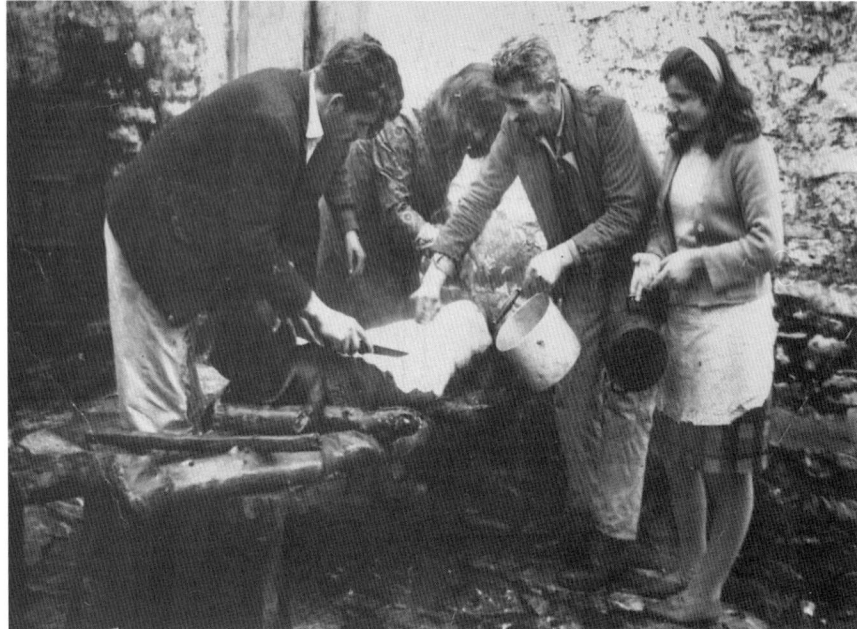

Christmas - 1966

Back to the Beginning

The majority of this book is composed of simple, fail-proof Greek recipes accompanied by photographs that are meant to inspire. These recipes will fit into your busy schedule. They will feed your busy family. They will help you entertain your friends. The traditional Greek kitchen is one of the healthiest in the world so you can proceed with a good conscience, keeping moderation in mind.

There are some recipes, like homemade phyllo and homemade sausages, that are time consuming and require some practice to perfect. We have placed these recipes in the section *Back to the Beginning*. We admit to not having made homemade phyllo or sausages prior to undertaking this book. We took on this challenge with levity. We wanted to affirm for ourselves that like our older relatives, we could perfect these back- to-the-basics recipes. We knew it would be satisfying to make our own sausages, and to serve them to our family knowing exactly what was in them.

We knew that the labour involved in rolling out our own phyllo would be worth it when we tasted the crunchy, yet delicate pastry, and proudly served it to others. What we didn't expect, and yet discovered with much delight, was that there was something else gained in the process of undertaking these more challenging recipes, something that has been lost in today's fast paced world.

The recipes in this section require a communal effort. They slow you down, they make you wait. And while you wait, you chat. And while you struggle, you laugh. And as you learn, you connect. We hope when the time is right, and you have assembled willing companions, friends and family, you slow down and go *Back to the Beginning* with them.

A NOTE ABOUT RECIPES

Before you get cooking please make note of the following things as we would like your experience in the kitchen to be as successful as possible.

Olive Oil always refers to Greek Extra Virgin Olive oil, unless otherwise specified.

Salt refers to coarse or fine sea salt.

Eggs are always large and organic. Eggs should be at room temperature before being used in any baking recipe.

Butter refers to salted butter, unless specified as unsalted.

Oven temperatures vary; so always check your meal a bit before the specified time. Always bake and roast in the centre of the oven unless otherwise specified.

Always read the entire recipe before beginning. Ensure that you have all of the ingredients and the proper equipment needed.

3 greek sisters

RECIPES-AT-A-GLANCE

We have found over the years that prep times vary from person to person. If the recipe is something you feel comfortable with, you may need little time to prep, whereas with a new recipe you may need some extra time to get it just right.

Some recipes also require many hours of waiting. You may need to wait a few hours for dough to rise, or you may need to wait overnight for raisins to soak in brandy. All this "time" needs to be taken into consideration when choosing a recipe. A cook needs to know how long it will take them from beginning to end; in other words, from the moment they choose a recipe to the moment the recipe is ready to be served to family and friends. We call this, *Time to Table*, and you will find that we've calculated this time for you at the bottom of every recipe in this cookbook. At-a-glance, you will now know how long each recipe will take accounting for all prep, rest, and cook times.

Also found at the bottom of each recipe is a bake temperature, a serving suggestion and a diet specification. Recipes with a "v" symbol are vegetarian recipes. Recipes with a "gf" symbol are gluten free. See sample recipe-at-a-glance below.

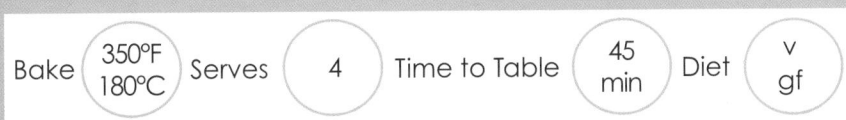

Also included after every recipe: make ahead suggestions, variations, tips, and substitutions.

Gluten-friendly recipes are also suggested as these recipes need only a small substitution to make them completely gluten-free.

food is love

In the Morning

Fried Egg
Strapatsada
Baklava French Toast
Apricot Jam
Orange Marmalade
Feta Biscuits
Greek Yogurt Smoothie
Breakfast Yogurt
Wheat Berry

FRIED EGG

Tiyanito Avgo (Tee-gah-nee-TOH Av-GOH)

Greek mothers do not fry their eggs in butter, rather, the eggs are bathed in a frying pan of hot olive oil. The oil needs to be so hot that you can hear the egg sizzle the instant it hits the frying pan and the edges of the egg-whites immediately turn a crispy brown. A spoon can be used to lap the oil over the top of the egg, so there is no need to turn it over.
In Greece, eggs are not just for breakfast, they are are a meal enjoyed anytime of day.

Ingredients
¼ cup olive oil
2 large eggs
Pinch of salt
Fresh cracked pepper
Mizithra cheese, grated
(optional)

1. Heat the olive oil in a frying pan over high heat. Crack the eggs into the hot oil and fry until the edges of the egg whites are golden and crispy. Use a spoon to scoop the olive oil over the egg yolk. Continue in this fashion until the yolk is cooked to your liking.

2. Remove from the heat and transfer the eggs to a plate along with some of the olive oil. Top with salt and pepper and serve. If desired, top with Mizithra cheese for a delicious finish.

I used to drive my mother crazy by leaving the whites of the egg in my plate as a child. One trip to Greece and one fried egg later, I was cured.
-Samantha

3 greek sisters

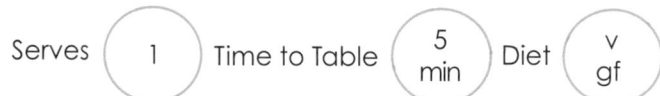
Serves (1) Time to Table (5 min) Diet (v gf)

STRAPATSADA

(Strah-pah-TSAH-dah)

If you plant tomatoes in the summer, there will come a time when you have more than you know what to do with. In our mom's village, Kastrougenna, the tomatoes were plentiful. This dish was a favourite as you need lots of tomatoes, and ripe ones. The ingredients are few in this dish, so the produce must be very good. Use a good extra-virgin Greek olive oil, ripe red tomatoes that still have the smell of summer on them, and large organic eggs.

1. Heat the olive oil in a large frying pan over medium heat. Add the tomatoes and cook gently until the tomatoes have broken down and completely absorbed their juices again, about 10-15 minutes.

2. In a small bowl, beat the eggs and salt together. Add to the pan with the thickened tomatoes and cook until the eggs have set. Serve immediately.

Ingredients
¼ cup olive oil
1 lb (500 g) vine-ripened tomatoes, chopped
4 eggs
Pinch of salt

Serves 2   Time to Table 15 min   Diet v gf

food is love

BAKLAVA FRENCH TOAST

In this decadent breakfast, we give French toast a classic Greek flair with ingredients such as, cinnamon, cloves, walnuts and honey. Perfect for Sunday brunch.

Ingredients
4 eggs, lightly beaten
¼ cup milk
¼ tsp salt
Olive oil for coating
8 thick slices of brown bread

For the Topping
1 cup walnut crumbs
1 tbsp sugar
1 tsp ground cinnamon
¼ tsp ground clove
Greek honey for drizzling

1. In a shallow bowl whisk the eggs, milk and salt together. Set this egg-mixture aside.

2. Coat the bottom of a frying pan with olive and heat over medium heat.

3. Dip the bread into the egg-mixture so that it is coated on both sides. Coat only enough slices of bread that can fit in your frying pan at one time to avoid soggy pieces.

4. Add the bread to the hot frying pan and cook until golden-brown on both sides, about 2 minutes per side.

5. Remove the bread from the pan and set aside in a warmed 200°F (93°C) oven, until ready to serve. Repeat with the remaining pieces of bread. Arrange the bread on a serving platter, and sprinkle with the walnut, sugar, cinnamon and clove topping. Drizzle with honey and serve.

Gluten Friendly
Use gluten-free bread to
enjoy this recipe.

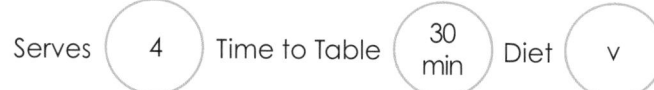

Serves (4) Time to Table (30 min) Diet (v)

3 greek sisters

Back to the Beginning

APRICOT JAM

Verikoka Marmalada (Veh-REE-koh-kah Mahr-mah-LAH-dah)

There is something magical about picking a ripe piece of fruit off a tree and eating it while it is still warm from the sun's rays. Several fruit trees can be found in Greece, among them, the bountiful apricot tree. Making an apricot jam is a great way to preserve the summer freshness of apricots. The apricot pit is easy to remove and the skin is left on the fruit during cooking, making this a choice fruit for preserving. Our recipe calls for less sugar than traditional jams, so you can feel good when having your second serving.

1 Slice the washed apricots in half and remove the pit.

2 Add the apricots and water to a medium saucepan and cook over medium heat until the apricots are soft and cooked through, about 5 minutes.

3 Add the sugar, stir to coat evenly, and bring mixture to a boil over medium-high heat. Continue boiling until mixture slightly thickens, about 5-10 minutes.

4 Remove from the heat, add the fresh lemon juice and stir. Transfer jam to sterilized jars and set aside to cool. Refrigerate until ready to serve.

Ingredients
1 lb (500 g) ripe apricots
¼ cup water
1½ cups sugar
1 tbsp fresh squeezed lemon juice

Make Ahead
Apricot jam can be stored in an airtight container and refrigerated for up to 6 months.

Sweetness
The amount of sugar suggested is a good starting point. Keep your own notes after you make it, and adjust the amount of sugar to suit your liking.

food is love

Makes (2 cups) Time to Table (30 min) Diet (v gf)

3 greek sisters

ORANGE MARMALADE

Marmalada Me Portokali (Mar-mah-LAH-dah Meh Pohr-toh-KAH-lee)

Making marmalade is like trapping sunshine in a jar. Oranges are plentiful at the grocery store during the winter months, and this is a great way to preserve them.

1. Peel the oranges and remove any seeds or white parts. Chop into small pieces and add to a medium saucepan. You should have about 3 cups chopped oranges. Sprinkle with sugar and mix to coat evenly.

2. Set the saucepan over high heat and bring to a boil. The oranges will release liquid. Once boiling, add the rinds and cinnamon stick and stir. Continue boiling over medium-high heat for 15 minutes.

3. Remove from the heat and set aside to cool. Transfer to a glass jar with a fitted lid and refrigerate until ready to serve.

Ingredients
6 oranges
1½ cups sugar
Rind of 1 orange, 1 lemon &
1 tangerine, chopped
¼ cinnamon stick

Taste
Be sure to use oranges that you enjoy eating, that way you are sure to enjoy the flavor of the marmalade. Sweetness is also a matter of taste; do adjust the amount of sugar to your liking.

Candy Thermometer
If using a candy thermometer, the marmalade must reach a jelling point of 220°F (104°C).

Tip
If you want to be doubly sure your marmalade is ready, place a small amount on a plate and refrigerate it until it's cool but not cold. If it is firm (not runny or hard) then it is ready.

Make Ahead
Marmalade can be stored in an airtight container and refrigerated for up to 1 month or in the freezer for up to 3 months.

food is love

Makes (2 cups) Time to Table (45 min) Diet (v gf)

3 greek sisters

FETA BISCUITS

Biscotta Me Feta (Bee-SKOH-tah Meh FEH-tah)

These feta biscuits are similar to tea biscuits in that they are made with flour and baking powder. The Greek difference is that they are loaded with the yummy goodness of feta cheese. Addictive!

1 In a large food processor add the flour, baking powder, salt, sugar and pulse 3 to 4 times to just mix the ingredients.

2 Add the butter and pulse until the butter breaks up into small crumb-like pieces, about 5 to 6 pulses.

3 Add the feta cheese and milk and pulse until the flour is moistened and a dough is about to form, about 5 to 6 pulses.

4 Transfer to a lightly floured work surface and gently knead the dough until it just comes together. Roll the dough into a flat disc about ½-inch (12 mm) to ¾-inch (18 mm) thick. Use a round 3-inch (7.5 cm) cutter to create small disc-shaped biscuits. Re-work the scraps of dough to create additional biscuits. Transfer biscuits to a parchment-paper lined baking sheet.

5 In a small bowl whisk the egg yolk and milk together, and use a pastry brush to brush the tops of each biscuit with this mixture. Place in the middle of a preheated oven for 15-18 minutes or until lightly golden in colour. Serve immediately or set aside to cool on a cooling rack.

Ingredients
2 cups all-purpose flour
2½ tsp baking powder
¼ tsp salt
1 tbsp sugar
6 tbsp cold unsalted butter, cut into ½-inch (12 mm) pieces
½ lb (250 g) feta cheese, crumbled
⅔ cup milk
Flour for dusting
1 egg yolk
2 tbsp milk

Make Ahead
Feta biscuits can be stored in an airtight container for up to 2 days and in a freezer for up to 2 months. Reheat in a 350°F (180°C) oven for 3-5 minutes from room temperature, or 15-20 minutes from frozen.

Bake (350°F 180°C) Makes (20-22) Time to Table (45 min) Diet (v)

food is love

GREEK YOGURT SMOOTHIE

If you are in a hurry and need to start your day off right, then a Greek yogurt smoothie with its high protein content is for you. Throw everything in a blender, mix and go!

Ingredients
½ cup blueberries or blackberries, frozen
½ cup milk
⅓ cup Greek yogurt
1 tbsp honey
Dash of cinnamon

1. Process the berries and milk in a food processor or blender and process until smooth, about 1 minute.

2. Add the yogurt, honey, and cinnamon and process briefly to combine. Pour into a glass and serve.

Substitutions
You do not have to limit yourself to frozen blueberries or blackberries. Any frozen fruit will do nicely here. Try strawberries, peaches, or raspberries. Fresh fruit is also suitable.

Variations
Give yourself an extra boost of protein, fibre and omega-3 by adding a teaspoon of Chia seeds to your smoothie. Chia seeds keep you full longer and will help you power through a busy day.

3 greek sisters

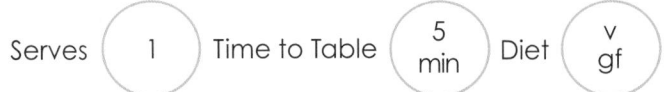
Serves 1   Time to Table 5 min   Diet v gf

BREAKFAST YOGURT

How wonderful to start your day with a meal that looks like dessert. Greek yogurt, both high in protein and low in fat, is the perfect start or end to any day.

Place the yogurt in a bowl and top with the peaches and walnuts. Drizzle with honey and enjoy.

Ingredients
¾ cup Greek yogurt
½ peach, sliced
1 tbsp walnuts, chopped
Drizzle of Greek honey

Substitutions
Fresh seasonal fruit such as apricots, peaches, bananas, berries, or apples.
Nuts such as pistachios, pecans, or almonds.

Variations
Dried fruit is also delicious, try apricots, cranberries or figs.

Homemade Yogurt
Head to page 224 for a recipe on how to make your very own homemade yogurt.

Serves 1   Time to Table 5 min   Diet v gf

food is love

3 greek sisters

Back to the Beginning

WHEAT BERRY

Sitari (See-TAH-ree)

Wheat berries make a wonderful snack - one that is both nutritious and delicious. The wheat berries are simply boiled and then dressed with nuts and raisins and lightly dusted with cinnamon and cloves. A sprinkling of sugar is also welcome.

1. Spread the wheat berry on a flat surface and check for small stones. Discard stones. Add the wheat berry to a pot of boiling water and boil for 15 minutes. Drain and replace with 5 cups water. Bring to a boil and continue boiling for 45 minutes. Remove the pot from the heat and set aside, covered, for one hour.

2. Drain the wheat berry and rinse under cold water. To remove the excess water, lay the berry on a clean kitchen towel and set aside for 10 minutes.

3. Add the wheat berry to a large bowl along with the rest of the ingredients, excluding the sugar. Mix and transfer to serving bowls. Sprinkle sugar to taste in each bowl and serve.

Ingredients
2 cups wheat berry
1 cup Sultana raisins
½ cup almonds, blanched & sliced
½ cup walnuts, chopped
½ cup sesame seeds, toasted
1 tsp coriander seeds, toasted & crushed
1 tsp ground cinnamon
½ tsp ground cloves
Sugar to taste

Koliva
Wheat berries are also used to prepare *Koliva*, a memorial food that is prepared by the family members of a loved one who has passed away. For this recipe see page 242.

Serves (8-10) Time to Table (2½ hours) Diet (v)

food is love

Know thyself - Socrates

To Start

Fiery Feta Dip
Almond Garlic Dip
Roasted Red Pepper Hummus
Eggplant Dip
Mussels Saganaki
Halloumi
Cheese Cigars
Crabcakes
Florina Roasted Peppers
Kale Chips
Warmed Citrus Olives
Shrimp Saganaki
Frappé

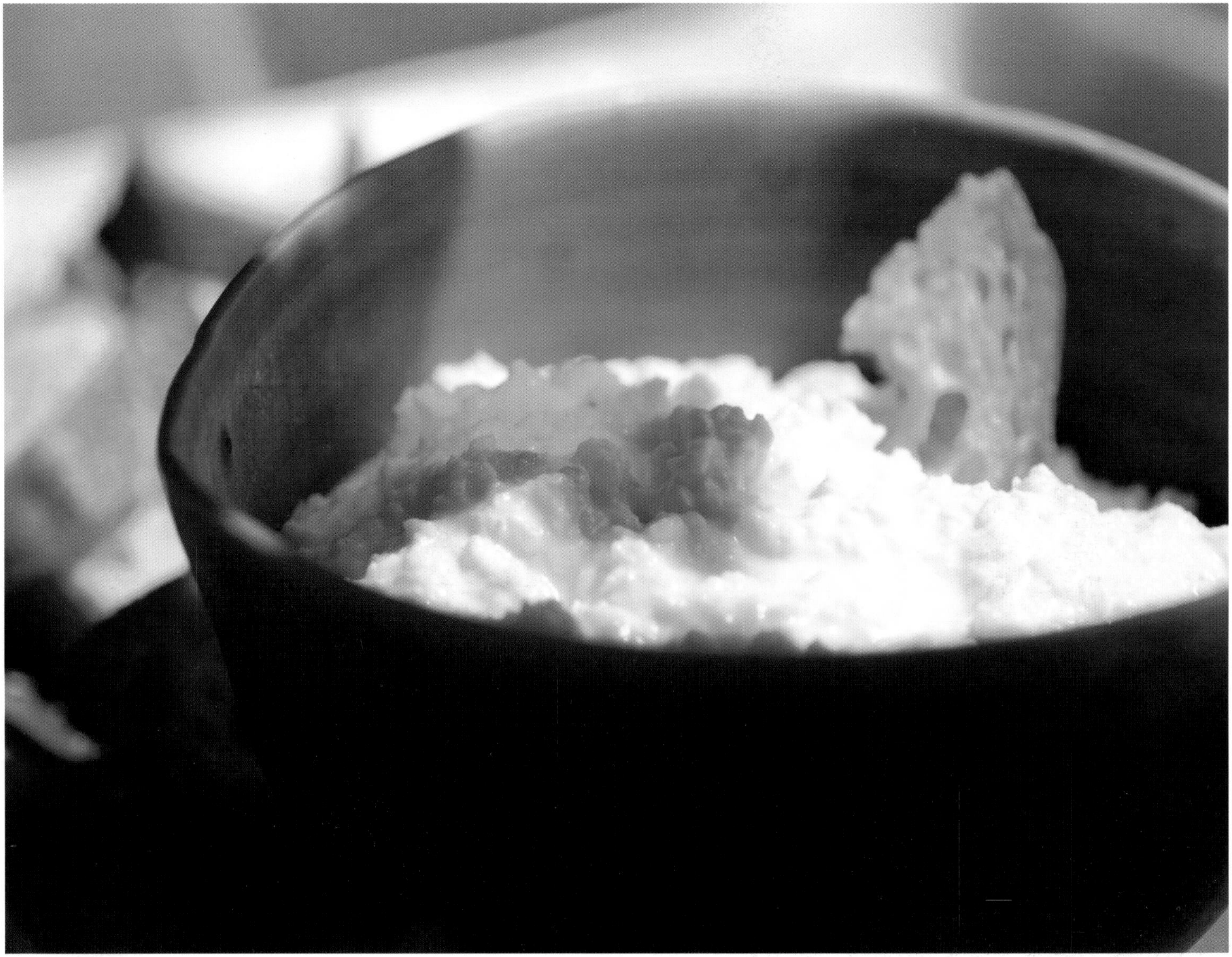

FIERY FETA DIP

Tirokafteri (TEE-roh-kah-fteh-ree)

Tirokafteri literally means spicy cheese, and the heat in this dish comes from a grilled hot banana pepper. It can be eaten as an appetizer with grilled pita wedges, bread sticks, or seasonal vegetables. It can also be used to spice up sandwiches. In Greece, this spread is offered at all sandwich bars.

1 Place the pepper whole on a preheated grill until the skin is charred on all sides, about 2 minutes per side. Set the pepper aside to cool for 10 minutes to allow the skin of the pepper to wrinkle. Peel and seed the pepper.

2 Process the pepper and remaining ingredients in a food processor until smooth and creamy. Serve.

Ingredients
1 hot yellow banana pepper
2 cups feta cheese, crumbled
½ cup Greek yogurt
4 tbsp olive oil

Tip
Yellow banana peppers are hot, so handle with care. Use gloves to remove the seeds. If your skin comes into contact with the seeds, wash thoroughly and avoid touching lips and eyes, as they will sting!

No Grill
Place the pepper on a baking sheet and directly under a broiler until the skin is blackened on all sides.

Make Ahead
Tirokafteri dip can be made up to 3 days in advance. Store in refrigerator until ready to serve.

Grill (High) Makes (2 cups) Time to Table (20 min) Diet (v gf)

food is love

3 greek sisters

ALMOND GARLIC DIP

Skordalia (Skor-tha-leeAH)

There are several versions of Skordalia in the Greek kitchen, with the varying ingredients being potatoes, bread and nuts. In all versions, however, garlic (in Greek, Skordo) is used. When served as a dip, Skordalia made with bread and almonds is our preferred recipe. This is a smooth and garlicky spread, perfect with bread sticks, vegetables, or grilled steak.

1. In a large bowl add the bread and water and set aside until the bread has absorbed the water, about 2 minutes.

2. Use your hands to squeeze the bread and remove as much of the water as possible.

3. Place the bread in a food processor, add the remaining ingredients and blend until smooth. Store in the refrigerator until ready to serve.

Ingredients
2 cups day-old white bread, crusts removed, cut into 2-inch (5 cm) cubes
1½ cups water
½ cup almonds, blanched
3 garlic cloves
½ cup olive oil
1 tbsp white wine vinegar
½ tsp salt

Make Ahead
Skordalia dip can be stored in an airtight container and refrigerated for up to 3 days in advance.

Substitution
Almonds can be substituted with walnuts or pine nuts.

Makes (1 cup)   Time to Table (15 min)   Diet (v)

food is love

3 greek sisters

ROASTED RED PEPPER HUMMUS

The culinary roots of hummus are not Greek. In Greece, chickpeas are most often eaten as a soup. Greek restaurants in North America, however, serve hummus alongside more traditional Greek dips, such as Tsatziki and Tirokafteri. We are simply addicted to hummus, so we thought we would include one of our favourite ways to smash chickpeas.

1. Place the pepper whole on a preheated grill until the skin is charred on all sides, about 2 minutes per side. Set the pepper aside to cool for 10 minutes to allow the skin of the pepper to wrinkle. Peel and seed the pepper.

2. Process the pepper and remaining ingredients in a food processor until smooth and creamy. Serve with pita chips or vegetables.

Ingredients
1 red bell pepper
1 can (19 oz/540 mL) chickpeas, drained and rinsed
3 tbsp fresh squeezed lemon juice
2 tbsp olive oil
1 tbsp tahini
1 garlic clove
¼ tsp salt

Variation
Dried chickpeas can be used in place of canned chickpeas. Simply soak 1 cup dried chickpeas in water overnight. Drain. Boil in 8 cups water until soft and cooked through.

Make Ahead
Roasted red-pepper hummus can be stored in an airtight container and refrigerated for up to 7 days in advance.

Tip
Roasted peppers can also be found in your grocery store in glass jars.

food is love

Grill (High) Makes (2 cups) Time to Table (20 min) Diet (v gf)

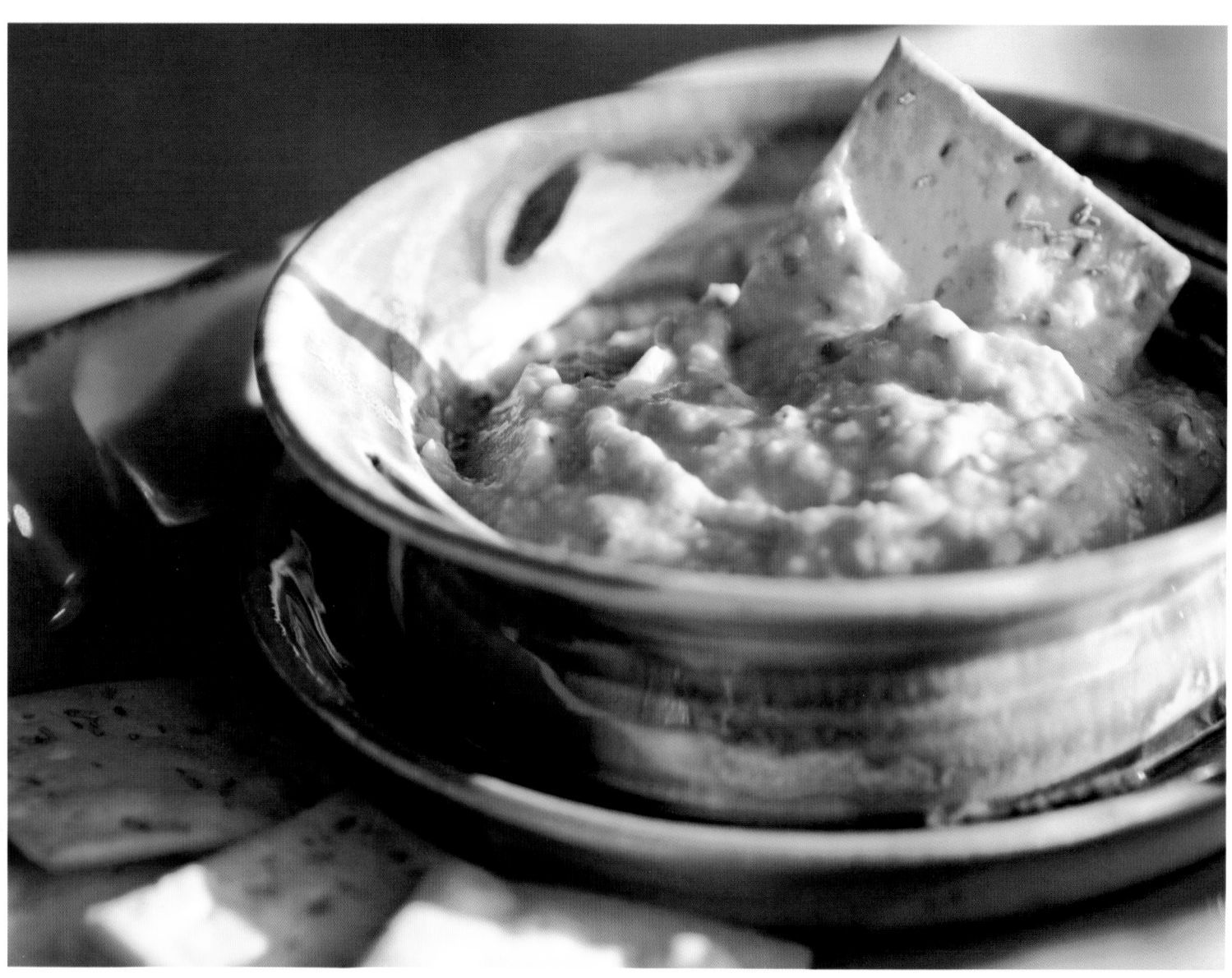

3 greek sisters

EGGPLANT DIP

Melitzanosalata (Meh-lee-dzah-noh-sah-LAH-tah)

In Greece, eggplant dip is known as Melitzanosalata, in the Middle East it is known as Baba Ghanouj. Essentially, it is a purée of eggplant and garlic with a little bit of tahini. It is both creamy and garlicky. In Greece, it is enjoyed seaside along with pita, cold beers and a variety of other appetizers and fish.

1. Use a fork to prick holes over the entire surface of the eggplant. Transfer to a baking sheet and place in the upper third of a preheated oven, until the skin is charred on all sides and the eggplant pulp is soft, about 30-45 minutes. Turn the eggplant every 10 minutes to ensure even cooking. Set eggplant aside to cool.

2. Cut the cooled eggplant in half and use a spoon to scoop out the flesh. Discard the skin. Place eggplant pulp in a food processor along with the remaining ingredients and process until smooth. Scrape down the sides of the bowl if necessary.

3. Transfer to a bowl and chill in refrigerator for at least one hour before serving.

Ingredients
1 large purple eggplant, about 1 lb (500 g)
3 tbsp fresh squeezed lemon juice
2 tbsp tahini
2 garlic cloves, minced
½ tsp salt

Tip
Once eggplant flesh is exposed to air it will turn a dark colour unless it is mixed with lemon juice. Add the eggplant pulp quickly to the lemon juice mixture once the eggplant has cooled to prevent discoloration.

Make Ahead
Eggplant dip can be stored in an airtight container and refrigerated for up to 7 days in advance.

food is love

Broil (High) Makes (3/4 cup) Time to Table (2 hours) Diet (v gf)

3 greek sisters

MUSSELS SAGANAKI

Midia Saganaki (MEE-dee-ah Sah-gah-NAH-kee)

Greece is surrounded by glorious blue water; the Aegean Sea on one side, and the Ionian Sea on the other. These waters provide Greeks and visitors an array of fish and shellfish to enjoy in the several tavernas that line the magnificent beaches. This was a beachside favourite, a quick lunch of mussels cooked in a spicy tomato sauce. You will need bread to sop up the juices in the bowl. Leave only the shells behind.

1 Wash the mussels thoroughly (see below) and set aside.

2 Heat the olive oil in a large pot over medium heat. Add the shallots, garlic and banana pepper and sauté until soft, about 2 minutes. Increase the heat to high, add the wine and reduce for 1 minute. Add the tomatoes, tomato paste, oregano and fresh cracked pepper and cook until tomatoes start to break down and release their juices, about 2 minutes.

3 Add the mussels to the pot and give them a quick stir. Cover and cook for 5 minutes. Remove the pot from the heat. Discard any mussels that did not open. Add the feta cheese, basil and serve immediately.

Ingredients
1 lb (500 g) mussels
2 tbsp olive oil
2 shallots, minced
4 garlic cloves, minced
1 yellow hot banana pepper, deseeded, finely chopped
½ cup white wine
2 plum tomatoes, chopped
1 tbsp tomato paste
¼ tsp dried oregano
Fresh cracked pepper
½ cup feta cheese, crumbled
2 tbsp fresh basil, minced

Cleaning Mussels
Mussels must be cleaned well just before cooking. To do this, rinse the mussels under cold water and remove any barnacles using a stiff brush. Cut or tug away any "beards". Place mussels in a sink filled with cold water and let them sit for 30 minutes so that any remaining sand or grit is removed. Drain and use immediately.

Mussels
Live mussels should be partially closed or completely closed. Discard any open or cracked mussel shells. If you are unsure about a mussel, tap it against a hard surface, if the mussel contracts and closes, it is alive.

Storing Mussels
Store mussels in a refrigerator until ready for use. Arrange in a bowl over ice or cover in a wet paper towel. Do not store in an airtight container as they will suffocate.

Serves 2 Time to Table 1 hour Diet v gf

food is love

3 greek sisters

HALLOUMI

(Hah-LOU-mee)

A tasty, salty and squeaky cheese made in Cyprus from sheep's and goat's milk. It is as readily available as Feta cheese and it can withstand very high temperatures making it an ideal cheese for grilling or frying. Try it on vegetarian skewers for added protein.

1. Heat a large skillet over high heat. Brush both sides of the halloumi cheese with olive oil and place in the hot skillet. Cook cheese on both sides until cheese has a golden-brown colour, about 1-2 minutes per side. Transfer grilled cheese to a serving platter.

2. In a separate small bowl whisk the vinaigrette ingredients together and drizzle over the cheese. Serve warm.

Ingredients
4 halloumi cheese slices,
¼-inch (6 mm) thick
Olive oil for greasing

For the Vinaigrette
2 tbsp olive oil
1 tbsp fresh squeezed lemon juice
1 tbsp fresh mint, minced
1 garlic clove, minced
1 fresh red chili pepper, deseeded, minced
2 Kalamata olives, sliced

Barbecue
Halloumi can also be grilled on a barbecue.

Serves	Time to Table	Diet
4	15 min	v gf

food is love

3 greek sisters

CHEESE CIGARS

Bourekakia Me Tiri (Boo-reh-KAH-kee-ah Meh Tee-REE)

These cheese-filled cigars are a tasty treat during a get-together. Yogurt and Mizithra are used as the filling in place of traditional feta cheese. The availability of thick Greek yogurt makes this a cinch to put together.

1. In a medium-sized bowl, mix the yogurt, Mizithra, olive oil and pepper together. This is the filling. Set aside.

2. In a small saucepan, melt the butter over low heat. Remove from the heat and skim away any foam. Use only clarified butter and avoid the white milk solids that have settled at the bottom of the pan.

3. Lay one phyllo sheet in front of you horizontally and cover the remaining sheets with a damp cloth to avoid drying out. Use a pastry brush to lightly brush the phyllo with some melted butter. Grab the right end of the phyllo sheet and fold the phyllo in half like a book. Lightly brush with some more butter.

4. Spoon 3 tablespoons of the filling along the narrow end of the phyllo leaving a ½-inch (12 mm) border. Fold the sides over to enclose the filling and roll up. Lay the cheese cigar in a 9-x13-inch (23x33 cm) buttered metal cake pan, seam-side down and brush the top with some butter. Do not overstuff each cigar as they will burst during cooking.

5. Place on a parchment-paper lined baking sheet and sprinkle with sesame seeds.

6. Repeat this process with the remaining sheets of phyllo.

7. Place the baking sheet in the middle of a preheated oven for 30 minutes or until golden-brown and crisp. Serve warm.

Ingredients
2 cups Greek yogurt
1½ cups Mizithra cheese, grated
2 tsp olive oil
¼ tsp black pepper
½ cup unsalted butter
10 prepared phyllo sheets, thawed at room temperature
¼ cup sesame seeds

Bake 350°F 180°C | Makes 10 | Time to Table 1 hour | Diet v

food is love

The flower that produces saffron, the crocus (Krokos), comes from Greece. Gathering the saffron is both labour intensive and time consuming, making saffron very expensive. Luckily you need only a pinch of saffron to impart the beautiful colour you are after in the Saffron Dipping Sauce.

Substitution
Lobster meat is the perfect substitute for crab meat.

CRABCAKES

Kavourokeftedes (Kah-vou-roh-keh-FTEH-des)

Greeks make lots of fried patties, fritters and cakes. They will shred just about any vegetable, mince any meat or fish, and turn them into delectable fried patties. Crab is no exception. On a recent trip to Greece we were quickly reminded why food is often fried. It is very hot in Greece, and frying is quick without the radiant heat of an oven. We find that cooking them in the oven gets them just as crispy, so we recommend baking them, as long as it's not 40 degrees outside!

1 Place the potatoes in a small pot, cover with water and bring to a boil. Continue boiling for 10 minutes. Remove from the heat and drain. Transfer to a large bowl and mash the potato.

2 Add the crab, bell pepper, chili pepper, chives, garlic, dill and dried seasonings to the large bowl with the mashed potato.

3 In a separate small bowl whisk the lemon, vinegar, oil, Dijon and egg together. Pour over the crab and use your hands to mix the ingredients thoroughly. Shape into 12 small patties and place on a well-greased baking sheet. Place in the middle of a preheated oven for 15 minutes.

4 Change oven temperature to broil and broil crab cake tops until golden brown, about 5 minutes. Transfer each crab cake to a serving platter with a spatula. Serve on their own or with Saffron Yogurt Dipping Sauce, see recipe below.

Ingredients
2 yellow potatoes, about ½ lb (250 g), peeled, cubed
1 lb (500 g) lump crab meat, well drained
1 yellow bell pepper, diced
½ red chili pepper, minced
¼ cup fresh chives, chopped
2 garlic cloves, minced
2 tbsp fresh dill, chopped
1 tsp dried oregano
1 tsp sweet paprika
¾ tsp salt
Juice of ½ lemon
3 tbsp balsamic vinegar
2 tbsp olive oil
1 tbsp Dijon mustard
1 egg
Olive oil for greasing

This is a bright, pretty, and refreshing dipping sauce, perfect for a rich crab cake.

Saffron Dipping Sauce

In a small bowl whisk the saffron powder and lemon juice together until the saffron has dissolved. Add the yogurt and salt and whisk until combined. Serve.

Makes (1/2 cup) Time to Table (10 min)

This dip can be stored in the refrigerator for up to 4-6 hours in advance.

Saffron Dipping Sauce
Pinch of saffron powder
2 tbsp fresh squeezed lemon juice
½ cup Greek yogurt
¼ tsp salt

Bake (425°F 220°C) Makes (12) Time to Table (1 hour) Diet (v gf)

food is love

3 greek sisters

Back to the Beginning

ROASTED FLORINA PEPPERS

Piperies Psites (Pee-phe-ree-EHS Psee-TEHS)

Sweet peppers from Florina (in Macedonia) are an integral part of the cuisine in Northern Greece. Florina peppers are bright red in colour, robust in flavour and subtly sweet. They can be fried, stuffed, grilled, or pickled. Shepperd peppers are similar to Florina peppers and can be found in late August in North America. When roasted, peppers gain a whole new depth of flavour which is only intensified when marinated with garlic, basil, olive oil and vinegar. They can be served as an appetizer, added to salads, pizza, sandwiches or pasta dishes.

1. Place the peppers whole on a preheated grill until the skin is charred on all sides, about 2 minutes per side. Set peppers aside to cool for 10 minutes to allow the skins of the peppers to wrinkle. Peel and seed the peppers.

2. Place the roasted peppers in a glass jar, add the remaining ingredients, place the lid on the jar and shake.

3. For best results, the peppers should marinate a couple of days before serving. Store in refrigerator. Bring back to room temperature before serving so that the olive oil liquefies once again.

Ingredients
6 whole red shepherd peppers
½ cup olive oil
¼ cup red wine vinegar
1 garlic clove, crushed
1 bay leaf
½ tsp salt
½ tsp dried oregano
½ tsp whole black peppercorns
¼ cup fresh basil, chopped

Make Ahead
Roasted peppers can be stored in an airtight container and refrigerated for up to 3 weeks in advance. Ensure that the peppers are completely covered in olive oil.

Substitution
Red bell peppers are a suitable substitute if long, narrow shepherd peppers cannot be found.

food is love

Grill (High) Makes (1 jar) Time to Table (2 days) Diet (v gf)

KALE CHIPS

A healthy chip? Yes! Kale chips are simple to make and they aren't fried. Although you should be forewarned: they are highly addictive.

Ingredients
1 bunch kale
¼ cup olive oil
¼ tsp salt

Variation
For a spicier kale chip, add cayenne or black pepper to the kale.

1. Trim stocks from ends of kale. Roughly chop kale greens. Wash kale greens thoroughly and pat dry with a paper towel or run through a salad spinner to remove excess water.

2. Drizzle kale with olive oil and use your hands to massage the oil into the kale to ensure that the kale is evenly coated. Arrange kale on a large baking sheet.

3. Sprinkle the kale with salt and place in the middle of a preheated oven for 7 minutes. Flip kale and cook for 3 minutes further, or until kale is crunchy. Serve immediately or let cool and serve at room temperature.

Bake (450°F / 230°C) Serves (2) Time to Table (20 min) Diet (v gf)

WARMED CITRUS OLIVES

Zestes Elies (Zeh-STES Eh-lee-EHS)

This is a nice way to introduce olives to a dinner party, served warm, with cocktails. They are great at the family dinner table too.

1. Place the ingredients in a small saucepan over low heat. Heat through, about 5 minutes. Transfer to a serving bowl.

2. Garnish with lemon and orange wedges and serve warm.

Ingredients
1 cup olives, choose a variety
½ cup olive oil
1 large strip orange rind
1 large strip lemon rind
2 garlic cloves, chopped
1 tsp fresh rosemary, chopped
¼ tsp dried red chilies

Garnish
Wedges of oranges and lemons

Makes (1 cup)   Time to Table (15 min)   Diet (v gf)

food is love

3 greek sisters

SHRIMP SAGANAKI

Garides Saganaki (Gah-REE-thes Sah-gah-NAH-kee)

If you find yourself screaming "Opa" while cooking, then you are probably making a saganaki dish, whether it is with cheese, shrimp or mussels. Serve this delicious appetizer with some baguette slices for a fabulous starter. This is a classic greek appetizer.

1. In a skillet, heat the olive oil over medium heat. Add the onion and sauté until soft, about 4 minutes. Add the garlic and chilies and cook for a minute further. Add the shrimp and cook until the shrimp are pink on both sides. Add the tomatoes and heat through. Stir in the tomato paste, salt and oregano and cook until the tomatoes break down and the sauce thickens, about 5 minutes.

2. Stir in the fresh parsley and basil and top with the crumbled feta. Place in the middle of a preheated oven for 5-10 minutes, or until the cheese is slightly brown and the sauce is bubbling hot.

3. Arrange the shrimp saganaki on baguette slices and serve.

Ingredients
2 tbsp olive oil
½ yellow onion, chopped
4 garlic cloves, sliced
½ tsp dried red chilies
12 shrimp, deveined and patted dry
2 vine-ripened tomatoes, diced
1 tbsp tomato paste
½ tsp salt
½ tsp dried oregano
¼ cup fresh parsley, chopped
¼ cup fresh basil, chopped
½ cup feta cheese, crumbled or Kefalotiri cheese, grated
½ baguette, sliced and lightly toasted

Gluten Friendly
Use gluten-free bread to enjoy this recipe.

Saganaki
Saganaki is a two-handled little frying pan.

food is love

Bake	400°F 200°C	Serves	2-3	Time to Table	50 min	Diet	v

3 greek sisters

FRAPPÉ

Coffee culture is alive and well in Greece. The cafés and outdoor bars are filled with people and lively conversations. To beat the heat people call for, "Frappé, se parakalo".

These foamy cold drinks, called frappé, are made from instant coffee. They have become an integral part of Greek culture. Instant coffee, sugar and water are mixed together and shaken with a hand mixer or a small electric mixer to form a thick foam. The foam is poured into a tall glass with cold water, ice cubes and evaporated milk, then served. "Efharisto!"

Cold water
Handful of ice cubes
1 tsp instant coffee
1 tsp sugar
2 tbsp evaporated milk

In a martini shaker or jar with a fitted lid add 2 tablespoons cold water, ice cubes, instant coffee, and sugar. Place the lid and shake vigorously for 10 seconds.

Pour the contents of the shaker into a tall water glass, add the milk and fill the remainder of the glass with cold water. Serve with a straw.

Note
Adjust the sugar to your liking.

food is love
After Dinner

The father crab watches his son walking and wonders to himself, why oh why can't he walk with his legs straight. So he tells his son, "Son, walk with your legs straight." To which the son responds, "Walk in front of me father and I shall walk just like you." So the father crab takes the lead. And the son follows. The father crab walks with his legs bent of course.

— Greek fable

Ο κάβουρας ορμήνευε το παιδάκι του, "Γιατί δεν μπορείς να περπατίσεις με τα πόδια σου ευθεία?"
Και ο κάβουρας απαντούσε, "Πήγαινε μπροστά και θα σε ακολουθήσω."

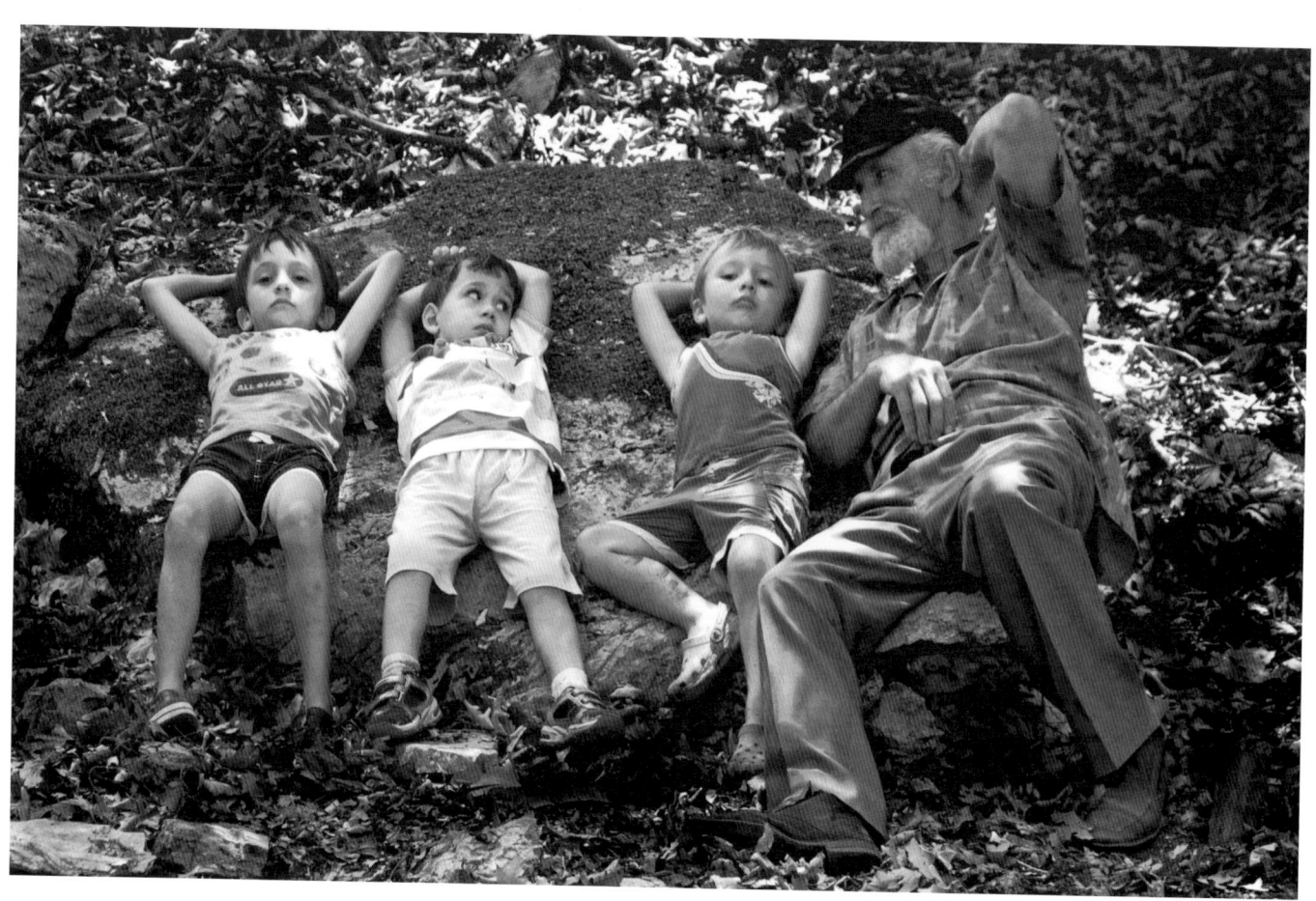

On the Side

Briami
Potato Salad
Fig & Walnut Salad
Watermelon Feta Salad
String Bean & Walnut Salad
Shrimp & Orzo Salad
Coleslaw
Bulgur Wheat Salad
Chickpea Salad with Mint & Yogurt
Broccoli with Lemon
Roasted Cauliflower
Red Lentil Soup - Two Ways
Santorini's Fava Soup
Fisherman's Soup

3 greek sisters

BRIAMI

(Bree-AH-me)

In Greece, vegetables are cooked beautifully, and the secret is that they are cooked seasonally and with plenty of flavourful extra-virgin olive oil. These dishes are referred to as Ladera, meaning lots of olive oil is used.
A walk through the garden in late summer would dictate what the Briami would consist of. Vegetables ready for picking would be harvested and tossed together with olive oil and seasonings. Beans, eggplant and zucchini make great additions to Briami. You will need approximately 3 lb (1½ kg) of seasonal vegetables. Below is only one possible combination. Change the vegetables to suit the season and your preference.

1. In an 11-inch (28 cm) square roasting pan toss the vegetables with the olive oil. Add the tomatoes and remaining seasonings.

2. Place in the middle of a preheated oven, uncovered, for 30 minutes.

3. Gently mix the vegetables so that they are once again coated with the olive oil and with the vegetable juices that have been released.

4. Continue cooking, covered, for 1 hour, or until the vegetables are soft and the juices have been reabsorbed. Serve hot or warm.

Ingredients
1 yellow onion, thinly sliced
¾ lb (350 g) green or yellow string beans, ends trimmed
6 garlic cloves, roughly chopped
2 yellow potatoes, peeled & cubed
3 zucchini, cut into 1-inch (2.5 cm) rounds
2 red bell peppers, roughly chopped
1 eggplant, cut into 2-inch (5 cm) pieces
½ cup olive oil
1 can (14 oz/398 mL) plum tomatoes, roughly chopped
1 tsp salt
1 tsp dried oregano
Fresh cracked pepper

food is love

| Bake | 425°F 220°C | Serves | 8 | Time to Table | 2 hours | Diet | v gf |

3 greek sisters

POTATO SALAD

Patatosalata (Pah-tah-toh-sah-LAH-tah)

Potato salads make great side dishes or light lunches. Make this a protein-rich meal by adding slices of hard-boiled eggs. This is also a great alternative to traditional potato salads that tend to be heavy on the mayonnaise.

1. In a large pot add the potatoes, salt and enough water to cover the potatoes. Bring to a boil and continue boiling until potatoes are fork tender, about 15 minutes. Drain and transfer potatoes to a large salad bowl. Add the remaining salad ingredients to the bowl.

2. In a separate small bowl, whisk the dressing ingredients together and drizzle dressing over potato salad. Toss salad and serve warm or cold.

Ingredients
6 large red potatoes,
about 3 lb (1½ kg), quartered
1 tsp salt
5 scallions, both white and
green parts, chopped
¼ cup capers
¼ cup fresh parsley, chopped
4 sprigs fresh thyme, chopped
10 cherry tomatoes, halved
10 Kalamata olives, pitted
Fresh cracked pepper

For the Dressing
⅓ cup olive oil
2 tbsp white wine vinegar
1 tsp grainy Dijon mustard
½ tsp salt

Serves 4 Time to Table 30 min Diet v gf

food is love

FIG & WALNUT SALAD

Salata Me Sika Ke Karidia (Sah-LAH-tah Meh SEE-kah Keh Kah-REE-dee-ah)

Fresh figs are sumptuous and a great addition to any summer salad. One of the joys of using seasonal fruit is that you will look forward to this salad when you begin seeing trays of figs arrive at the grocers. This salad has many Greek elements: the honey, the balsamic vinegar, the Manouri cheese, the walnuts and of course the ripe figs.

Ingredients
For the Dressing
¼ cup olive oil
2 tbsp Greek balsamic vinegar
1 tbsp Greek honey
¼ tsp each salt & pepper

For the Salad
6 cups mixed greens
4 figs, quartered
8 slices Manouri cheese,
¼-inch (6 mm) thick
¼ cup walnuts, roughly
chopped

1. Mix the dressing together and set aside.

2. Add the mixed greens to a large bowl. Drizzle the dressing on the greens and toss well.

3. Divide the greens on individual salad plates. Top each salad off with the fresh figs, cheese and walnuts.

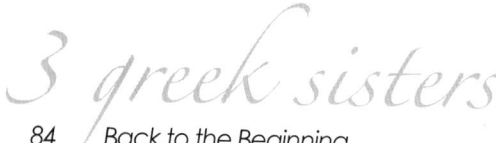
3 greek sisters

Serves 4 Time to Table 15 min Diet v gf

WATERMELON FETA SALAD

Karpouzosalata (Kahr-pou-zo-sah-LAH-tah)

A colourful and refreshing salad that will both surprise and please. The sweetness of a good quality balsamic vinegar compliments feta cheese very nicely. Bursts of fresh mint combined with quenching watermelon awaken your tastebuds.

1 Add the watermelon, feta and mint to a salad bowl.

2 In a separate small bowl whisk the dressing ingredients together. Pour over the salad just before serving.

Ingredients
2 cups seedless watermelon, cubed
½ cup feta cheese, cubed
¼ cup fresh mint, finely chopped

For the Dressing
¼ cup olive oil
2 tbsp balsamic vinegar
¼ tsp salt
Fresh cracked pepper, if desired

Serves (4) Time to Table (15 min) Diet (v gf)

food is love

3 greek sisters

STRING BEAN & WALNUT SALAD

Fassolakia Me Karidia (Fah-soh-LAH-kee-ah Meh Kah-REE-dee-ah)

The beans in this salad are cooked through, yet crunchy. They are simply dressed with honey, walnuts and cherry tomatoes. Beautiful to behold and a great make-ahead salad.

1. Add the string beans to a pot of salted boiling water for 8 minutes. Drain the beans and run under cold water to stop the beans from cooking further.

2. Transfer the beans to a salad bowl. Add the walnuts, tomatoes and onions to the salad bowl.

3. In a separate small bowl, whisk the dressing ingredients together and pour over the bean salad. Toss and serve.

Ingredients
1 lb (500 g) green string beans, ends trimmed
½ cup walnuts, chopped
20 cherry tomatoes
½ red onion, thinly sliced

For the Dressing
¼ cup olive oil
2 tbsp red wine vinegar
1 tsp Dijon mustard
1 tbsp Greek honey
½ tsp dried oregano
¼ tsp salt

Make Ahead
This salad can be made and stored in the refrigerator up to 1-day in advance.

Serves (4) Time to Table (25 min) Diet (v gf)

food is love

3 greek sisters

SHRIMP & ORZO SALAD

Kritharaki Me Garides (Kree-thah-RAH-kee Meh Gah-REE-des)

Serve this on its own for a light lunch, or add it to a buffet for an impressive presentation. The shrimp have just a bit of a kick, just enough to keep you coming back for more. The key to success for this salad is in the orzo – if cooked too long, the dressing will make it soggy, if the orzo isn't cooked long enough, it will stick to your teeth. See below for perfect results.

1. Bring a large pot of water to a boil. Add the orzo and a pinch of salt and cook for 13-15 minutes. Drain orzo and place in serving bowl.

2. Whisk the dressing ingredients together and pour over the cooked orzo. Stir the orzo and set aside to cool.

3. Once the orzo has cooled, add the tomatoes, peppers, scallions, and basil and mix.

4. Rinse the shrimp under cold water and pat dry with a paper towel. Lightly coat the shrimp in olive oil. Add a squeeze of lemon juice to the shrimp and season with salt, cayenne pepper, oregano and fresh cracked black pepper. Toss the shrimp to ensure that they are seasoned evenly. Add the shrimp to the orzo salad.

5. Top the salad with the crumbled feta cheese, mix gently and serve.

Perfect Orzo
Greek orzo is firmer in texture and needs to cook a little longer than other orzo. At about 13 minutes begin checking the orzo. It should be only slightly firm or al dente. You should be able to bite through the orzo without it sticking to your teeth. If it is still hard, cook a couple of minutes longer. Keep an eye on it, when ready, remove and put in colander to drain water immediately. Once the dressing is added, it will expand further.

Make Ahead
Shrimp & Orzo Salad can be made and stored in the refrigerator on the morning of serving day.

Ingredients
1½ cups Greek orzo
Pinch of salt

For the Dressing
⅓ cup olive oil
1 tbsp fresh squeezed lemon juice
2 tbsp white wine vinegar
1 tsp Dijon mustard
2 garlic cloves, minced
¼ tsp salt

For the Salad
10 cherry tomatoes
1 orange bell pepper, thinly sliced
2 hot banana peppers, thinly sliced
5 scallions, both white & green parts, chopped
¼ cup fresh basil, minced
1 lb (500 g) thawed, cooked & peeled cold-water shrimp (150-200 shrimp count)
Olive oil for coating
Squeeze of lemon juice
¼ tsp salt
¼ tsp cayenne pepper
¼ tsp dried oregano
Fresh ground black pepper
1 cup feta cheese, crumbled

food is love

Serves (6) Time to Table (45 min) Diet (v)

3 greek sisters

COLESLAW

Maposalata (Ma-poh-sah-LAH-tah)

Shredding cabbage takes patience – so naturally, these tasks were passed over to our dad. Our dad is a man with a lot of patience, he raised three daughters after all. He relishes making maposalata. With a glass of his homemade wine by his side, and Greek tunes playing in the background, he patiently shreds the cabbage and the carrots with his beloved mandoline. The dressing is always simple: olive oil, lemon juice and salt. Maposalata was always served alongside grilled meats, especially our lamb burgers. For large gatherings, simply double.

1. Add the shredded cabbage and carrots to a large bowl.

2. Whisk the dressing ingredients together in a small bowl. Pour over the cabbage and carrots and mix well. Store the coleslaw in the refrigerator until ready to serve.

Ingredients
½ cabbage head, about 4 cups, shredded
6 carrots, peeled, about 2 cups, shredded

For the Dressing
½ cup olive oil
¼ cup fresh squeezed lemon juice
1 tbsp sugar
1 tsp salt
Fresh cracked pepper

Make Ahead
Coleslaw can be prepared and stored in the refrigerator for up to 3 days in advance.

Serves 6   Time to Table 30 min   Diet v gf

food is love

BULGUR WHEAT SALAD

Salata me Pligouri (Sah-LAH-ta meh Plee-GOU-ree)

Bulgur wheat is high in fibre and has a slightly nutty flavour. In this dish, fresh chopped herbs and lemon juice transform bulgur into a refreshing, flavourful salad. This salad is a great make-ahead salad, as time will simply let all the flavours come together.

Ingredients
2 cups water
1 cup bulgur wheat
½ tsp salt
2 tomatoes, chopped
5 scallions, white and pale green parts, chopped
¼ cup each of fresh parsley, mint and oregano, minced
Fresh cracked pepper

For the Dressing
5 tbsp fresh squeezed lemon juice
¼ cup olive oil
¼ tsp salt

1. Bring 2 cups water to a boil in a medium pot over high heat. Add the bulgur wheat and salt. Remove from heat and set aside, covered, for 1 hour, or until all of the water has been absorbed.

2. Fluff the cooked bulgur wheat with a fork and transfer to a medium-sized bowl. Add the tomatoes, scallions, herbs and pepper and mix.

3. Add the dressing ingredients to a small bowl and whisk. Drizzle over the bulgur wheat salad and mix thoroughly. Serve right away or let the salad sit and marinate for a couple of hours before serving.

Optional
For added texture, add crumbled crispy pita chips to the salad just before serving.

Make Ahead
This salad can be made one day ahead and served cold.

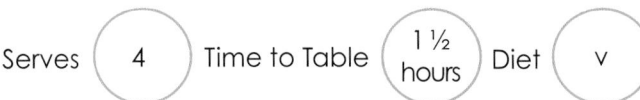

3 greek sisters

Serves (4) Time to Table (1 ½ hours) Diet (v)

food is love

3 greek sisters

CHICKPEA SALAD WITH MINT & YOGURT

Revithosalata (Reh-vee-tho-sah-LAH-tah)

Cold weather calls for warm salads. This chickpea salad with allspice and cumin is very fragrant and colourful. The mint is playful on the palate. Very yummy and comforting.

1. Heat 2 tablespoons of the olive oil in a large saucepan over medium heat. When the oil is hot, add the cumin and chilies and cook, stirring constantly, until the seeds are toasted, about one minute. Add the remaining olive oil along with the scallions and garlic and sauté for about 2 minutes, ensuring that the garlic does not brown. Add the tomatoes, chickpeas, salt and allspice, stir and cook until the chickpeas are warmed and the tomatoes have broken down and absorbed their juices, about 5 minutes.

2. Remove from the heat and stir in the fresh mint. Taste and adjust the seasonings if necessary. Transfer to serving bowls and top with a dollop of Greek yogurt. Serve.

Ingredients
- ¼ cup olive oil
- 1 tbsp whole cumin seeds
- ¼ tsp dried red chilies
- 5 scallions, white and pale green parts, chopped
- 2 garlic cloves, chopped
- 3 vine-ripened tomatoes, chopped
- 1 can (19 oz/540 mL) chickpeas, drained and rinsed
- ¼ tsp salt
- ¼ tsp ground allspice
- ¼ cup fresh mint, minced
- 4 tbsp Greek yogurt

Serves 4   Time to Table 20 min   Diet v gf

food is love

BROCCOLI WITH LEMON

Broccolo Me Lemoni (BRO-ko-lo Me Le-MOH-nee)

There is no need to drown broccoli in cheese for it to taste good. A simple dash of lemon and oil brightens up any dish. Although simple to make, broccoli can easily overcook. Our tip is to add the broccoli florets to boiling water with the florets facing up and slightly out of the water. A timer is also a good idea - since getting distracted in the kitchen is pretty easy to do.

Ingredients
1 head of broccoli
Salt
3 tbsp olive oil
Lemon wedges

1 Remove the main broccoli stem and cut the broccoli into small florets. Rinse and set aside.

2 Bring a large pot of salted water to a boil. Add the broccoli to the boiling water, stalks down and florets facing up. Once the water reaches a boil again, blanch for 3 minutes further.

3 Drain and arrange on a platter. Sprinkle with more salt if desired. Drizzle with olive oil and fresh-squeezed lemon juice just before serving.

3 greek sisters

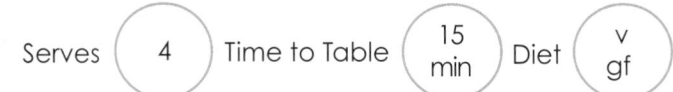
Serves 4   Time to Table 15 min   Diet v gf

ROASTED CAULIFLOWER

Kounoupidi Sto Fourno (Kou-nou-PEE-dee Stoh FOUR-noh)

In Greece, cauliflower is often enjoyed in the same way as broccoli, boiled with a drizzle of lemon juice and olive oil. As kids we would often complain of how stinky the house would smell after our parents boiled this autumn vegetable. Nowadays in our own kitchens, we love roasting cauliflower. Roasting intensifies the flavour of cauliflower, while emitting a pleasant aroma. The crispy cheese topping makes for a fancy presentation, plus, who doesn't like crisped cheese?

1 Cut the cauliflower into florets and place in a large bowl. Add the garlic, olive oil and toss to coat the cauliflower.

2 Transfer cauliflower to a baking sheet. Squeeze the lemon juice over the cauliflower and sprinkle with salt.

3 Top with the grated cheese and place in the middle of a preheated oven for 25-30 minutes, or until the cauliflower is lightly browned and can be easily pierced with a fork. Serve.

Ingredients
1 head of cauliflower
3 garlic cloves, minced
¼ cup olive oil
Juice of ½ lemon
¼ tsp salt
½ cup Kefalotiri or Kasseri cheese, grated

Substitution
Greek Kefalotiri or Kasseri cheese can be substituted with Parmesan cheese.

Bake 400°F 200°C Serves 4 Time to Table 40 min Diet v gf

food is love

In this Photograph
A small sweet potato was cut into the size of
matchsticks and fried in hot olive oil until crispy.

3 greek sisters

RED LENTIL SOUP - TWO WAYS

Kokkines Fakies (KOH-kee-nes Fah-kee-ES)

This recipe adds a non-traditional ingredient to a traditional soup. A sweet potato is added to a wholesome pot of red lentils and the result is a deliciously creamy soup with just a subtle hint of sweetness.
We have also included the traditional version for those who enjoy a splash of vinegar with their lentils. Both soups are easy and satisfying.

Ingredients
1½ cups red lentils
3 tbsp olive oil
1 yellow onion, minced
2 carrots, peeled, chopped
2 celery stalks, chopped
2 garlic cloves, minced
1 sweet potato, peeled & cut into small pieces
½ tsp dried red chilies
1 can (14oz/398mL) plum tomatoes, chopped
6 cups water
1½ tsp salt
½ tsp dried oregano
2 bay leaves

1   Wash the red lentils under cold running water until the water runs clear. Set aside.

2   Heat the olive oil in a large pot over medium heat. Add the onion, carrots and celery and sauté until soft, about 5 minutes. Add the garlic, sweet potato and chilies and sauté a minute further. Add the red lentils, tomatoes, water, salt, oregano and bay leaves and bring to a boil over high heat. Reduce the heat and simmer for 30 minutes, or until the sweet potato and lentils are cooked through.

3   Remove from the heat and discard the bay leaves. Purée the soup using a food processor or immersion blender.

4   Ladle individual portions of soup and serve with rustic bread.

Traditional Lentil Soup
For a traditional red lentil soup, simply omit the sweet potato. Once the soup is cooked, remove the bay leaves, and add ¼ cup chopped parsley. Ladle individual portions of soup and finish with a splash of red wine vinegar and a drizzle of olive oil.

Serves (6)   Time to Table (1 hour)   Diet (v gf)

food is love

3 greek sisters

SANTORINI'S FAVA SOUP

Fava (FAH-vah)

We first tried fava soup on the sun-soaked island of Santorini. Santorini fava, a yellow split pea variety, has been growing on the volcanic island for thousands of years. We remember it as a creamy purée with very few ingredients added: an onion, olive oil, salt and water. These few and humble ingredients made for a satisfying soup. In this recipe, however, we have added a few more ingredients and some finishing touches to make it a showstopper.

1. Heat the olive oil in a large pot over medium heat. Add the onion and sauté until soft, about 2 minutes. Add the carrot, celery and garlic and sauté for a minute further. Add the split peas, water, bay leaf and salt and bring to a boil over high heat. Reduce the heat and simmer, partially covered, until the split peas break down and the water has reduced, about 40-45 minutes. If the soup has thickened before the peas have cooked, add an additional 1-2 cups water and continue simmering.

2. Remove from the heat and discard the bay leaf. Purée the soup using a food processor or immersion blender.

3. Ladle individual portions of soup and drizzle each bowl with olive oil and a squeeze of lemon juice. Garnish with some red onion, a dollop of yogurt, some parsley and coarse finishing salt. Serve warm.

Ingredients
3 tbsp olive oil
1 yellow onion, chopped
1 carrot, peeled, chopped
1 celery, chopped
3 garlic cloves, chopped
2 cups yellow split peas
7 cups water
1 bay leaf
1½ tsp salt

Garnish
Olive oil for drizzling
Lemon wedges
½ red onion, diced
Greek yogurt
Fresh parsley, chopped
Coarse finishing salt

Make Ahead
This soup can be made up to 2 days in advance. As the soup sits, it continues to thicken. Simply add more water to the soup and then reheat before serving. Add garnish ingredients to each bowl when ready to serve.

Serves 4   Time to Table 1 hour   Diet v gf

food is love

Variation
Haddock, red snapper, white grouper, or red mullet can be used instead of sea bream.

3 greek sisters

FISHERMAN'S SOUP

Kakavia (Kah-kah-vee-AH)

Kakavia is to Greeks what bouillabaisse is to the French. It is a fisherman's soup, or Psarosoupa, a soup traditionally made with the varied bounty of a day out at sea. Whatever was caught in the net, ended up in the "kakavi", or the pot used to make the soup. We make this soup with fish we "catch" at our local fishmonger. Remember that the fish needs to be fresh, and the soup should be made up of seafood you enjoy eating. Below is our favourite combination of seafood, but changing the fish to suit your liking is completely encouraged.

Ingredients
1 lb (500 g) mussels
1 lb (500 g) clams
1 lb (500 g) shrimp, with the shells
1 lb (500 g) sea bream
¼ cup olive oil
3 leeks, white & pale green parts, thinly sliced
3 carrots, peeled, chopped
3 celery stalks, chopped
5 garlic cloves, minced
1 bay leaf
¾ tsp dried red chilies
1¼ tsp salt
Fresh ground pepper
1 tbsp tomato paste
¼ cup Cognac
1 cup white wine
1 can (14 oz/398 mL) plum tomatoes
5 cups water
3 small yellow potatoes, peeled, cut into 1-inch (2.5 cm) cubes
¼ cup fresh parsley, chopped
Juice of ½ lemon

1. Rinse the mussels under cold water. Scrub the shells thoroughly and remove the beards. Set aside to soak in cold water for 30 minutes to remove any grit. Meanwhile, rinse the clams under cold water. Scrub the shells and set aside. Remove the shells of the shrimp and place them in a small cheesecloth. Secure the cheesecloth with cooking string and set aside. Place the peeled shrimp in cold water and set aside. Cut the sea bream into 2-inch (5 cm) pieces and set aside.

2. Heat the olive oil in a large pot over medium heat. Add the leeks, carrots and celery and sauté until softened, about 5-7 minutes. Add the garlic and continue cooking for a minute further. Add the bay leaf, chilies, salt, pepper, tomato paste, and give it a good stir.

3. Increase the heat to high, add the Cognac and cook for a minute further. Add the wine, bring to a boil, and let it reduce by half.

4. In a blender or food processor add the canned tomatoes and process until smooth. Add it to the pot along with the shrimp shells in the cheesecloth and the water. Bring the ingredients to a boil, lower the heat and low-boil, uncovered, for 30 minutes.

5. Discard the cheesecloth with the shrimp shells.

6. Add the potatoes and the clams to the pot and continue simmering, covered, for 10 minutes.

7. Add the mussels, shrimp, and sea bream to the pot and continue simmering, covered, for 10 minutes. Remove and discard the bay leaf, and any mussels or clams that have not opened. Add the parsley and lemon juice to the pot and stir. Serve.

Serves (6-8) Time to Table (2 hours) Diet (v gf)

food is love

For Dinner

Creamy Yogurt Chicken
Chicken with Egg Noodles
Braised Chicken & Okra
Grilled Lemon Chicken
Chicken & Leek Pie Filling

Fennel Ribs
Kreatopita Pie Filling
Sofrito
Spetzofai

Lamb Fricassee with Dill & Greens
Lamb Burgers
Lamb Chops with Brandy Mint Sauce
Lamb Shanks
Kleftiko

Dinner Continued

Meatloaf
Soutzoukakia
Beef Barley & Olive Stew
Stuffed Cabbage Rolls with a Lemon Finish

Smelts
Cod Burgers
Baked Cod Casserole

Chestnut Stifado
Lentil Burgers
Leek Pie Filling

3 greek sisters

CREAMY YOGURT CHICKEN

Kota Me Yiaourti (KOH-tah Meh Yee-ah-OOR-tee)

This dish is so rustic and Greek. Seasoned yogurt is added to seared chicken breasts and baked. Once baked, yogurt resembles ricotta cheese, but is much more flavourful. The result is a creamy dish that is delectable. This recipe cooks best in stoneware.

1 In a non-reactive glass bowl, whisk the yogurt, eggs, garlic, mint, paprika, salt and pepper together. Set aside.

2 Coat the chicken in olive oil and season with salt and pepper.

3 Heat a skillet large enough for all six pieces of chicken over high heat. Add the chicken to the skillet and sear until lightly browned, about 2 minutes per side.

4 Remove the skillet from the heat. Pour the yogurt mixture set aside earlier directly into the skillet. Smooth with a rubber spatula and ensure that all pieces of chicken are completely covered in the yogurt mixture. Top with the grated cheese and place the skillet in the middle of a preheated oven for 20 minutes, or until the chicken is cooked through and the cheese is melted and golden. Serve hot.

Ingredients
2 cups Greek yogurt
2 eggs, lightly beaten
4 garlic cloves, minced
¼ cup fresh mint, chopped
1 tsp sweet paprika
¼ tsp salt
Fresh cracked pepper
6 chicken breasts, boneless, skinless
Olive oil for coating
½ tsp salt
Fresh cracked pepper
½ cup Kefalotiri cheese, grated

Substitution
Kefalotiri cheese can be substituted with Parmesan cheese.

food is love

| Bake | 425°F 220°C | Serves | 6 | Time to Table | 45 min | Diet | gf |

Homemade Egg Noodles
Head to page 221 for a recipe on how to make your
very own homemade egg noodles.

3 greek sisters

CHICKEN WITH EGG NOODLES

Kota Me Hilopites (KOH-tah Meh Hee-loh-PEE-tehs)

It was quite common back in the day to braise a large rooster or hen in a pot with cinnamon and tomatoes. This dish was often chosen for large gatherings, both for its simplicity and ability to feed a lot of people. Bellies were made full with the addition of homemade hilopites or egg noodles.

1. Prepare the whole chicken into serving pieces of roughly the same size. The breasts should be cut in two, the thighs should be separated from the legs and the wing tips should be removed and discarded. Remove the skin from the chicken pieces and discard. Add ½ tsp of the salt and some fresh cracked pepper to the chicken.

2. Heat the olive oil in a large pot over high heat. Reduce the heat to medium-high and add the onion. Sauté until soft, about 5 minutes. Add the chicken and cook about 2 minutes per side. The chicken will sweat and whiten as it cooks.

3. Add the chopped tomatoes, cinnamon stick and cloves and give it a good stir. Sauté until the tomatoes begin to break down, about 2 minutes.

4. In a cup, dilute the tomato paste with the warm water and add it to the pot along with the remaining salt.

5. Bring the ingredients to a boil over high heat. Reduce the heat and simmer, covered, for 1 hour, or until the chicken is cooked through.

6. Remove the chicken pieces with a slotted spoon and transfer to a plate. Set aside. Add the 2 cups boiling water with a pinch of salt to the pot, increase the heat to high and bring to a boil. Add the egg noodles, reduce the heat to medium and cook for 5 minutes or until the noodles are soft and cooked.

7. Remove the pot from the heat and return the chicken to the pot. Give it a quick stir and serve.

If desired, top each serving plate with grated mizithra cheese.

Ingredients
1 chicken, 3 lb (1½ kg), cut into serving pieces, skin removed
1 tsp salt
Fresh cracked pepper
¼ cup olive oil
1 yellow onion, minced
3 Roma tomatoes, chopped
½ cinnamon stick
5 cloves
2 tbsp tomato paste
2 cups warm water
2 cups boiling water
Pinch of salt
2 cups egg noodles
Optional
Mizitha cheese, grated (optional)

Tomato Peel
If you do not like tomato peel in your sauce, then simply blanch the tomatoes before adding them to the pot. Use a knife to mark the bottom of each tomato with an "X", drop into a pot of boiling water, remove after 5 minutes with a slotted spoon, and peel tomato skin when cool.

food is love

Serves (4) Time to Table (2 hours)

BRAISED CHICKEN & OKRA

Kokkinisti Kota Me Bamies (Koh-kee-nee-STEE KOH-tah Meh BAM-ee-ehs)

Okra, also known as lady's fingers, are too often a neglected ingredient, but they are the stars of this humble dish. Okra, a highly nutritious vegetable, is prepared with extra virgin olive oil, tomatoes, and chicken. When using few ingredients, as we have in this recipe, the individual components need to be exceptional. Use only fresh, young okra.

Ingredients
¼ cup olive oil
1 yellow onion, minced
4 chicken breasts, bone-in, skinless
1 can (28 oz/796 mL) plum tomatoes, roughly chopped
1 tbsp tomato paste
½ cup water
1 tsp salt
Fresh cracked pepper
¾ lb (350 g) fresh or frozen okra, ends trimmed

1. Heat the olive oil in a large pot over medium heat. Add the onion and sauté until soft, about 5 minutes. Add the chicken to the pot and cook, about 2 minutes per side. The chicken is ready to be turned over when it pulls away from the pot easily. If the chicken sticks, continue cooking a minute further. The chicken will sweat and whiten as it cooks.

2. Add the remaining ingredients except for the okra and mix the ingredients together. Bring to a boil, reduce the heat to medium and low-boil, partially covered, for 1 hour.

3. Carefully add the okra so that all the okra is immersed in cooking liquid. While the dish is cooking, avoid stirring, as this will pierce the okra. Use the handles of the pot to the move the ingredients around in the pot if required.

4. Continue cooking over medium heat, partially covered, for 30 minutes, or until the okra is soft and the chicken is cooked. Serve.

Okra
Okra is green and fuzzy, with an elongated shape. The inside is full of tiny seeds and a slimy, sticky substance. This natural sticky substance is the thickening agent used in many southern gumbo dishes. Okra tastes great when young and fresh, with no bruising. If you cannot find fresh okra that is tender, then frozen okra is perfectly acceptable, and sometimes preferred.

3 greek sisters

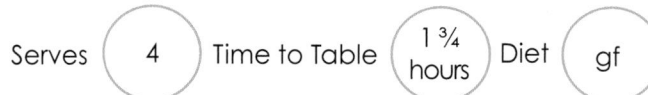

Serves (4) Time to Table (1 ¾ hours) Diet (gf)

As a kid I never had a problem eating all my vegetables, and okra was no different. Plus, I loved the glowing praise I would get from my parents for eating all my veggies!
- Betty

food is love

3 greek sisters

GRILLED LEMON CHICKEN

Kota Psiti Me Lemoni (KOH-ta Psee-TEE Meh Leh-MOH-nee)

Grilling meats is a specialty of almost all Greek dads. Our dad loves any excuse to fire up the BBQ. Here is a simple way to cook chicken perfectly every time. The magic is in the dressing.

1. Coat the chicken on both sides with the olive oil and season with salt, oregano and pepper.

2. Place the chicken directly on the grill and grill for 8-12 minutes, or until the chicken is firm to the touch and opaque all the way through. Ensure that the barbecue lid is closed as much as possible while cooking, and turn the breasts over only once.

3. Remove chicken from the grill, cover with aluminum foil and set aside to rest for 5 minutes.

4. Meanwhile, whisk the dressing ingredients together.

5. Use a sharp knife to cut the chicken into slices. Drizzle the dressing over the chicken and serve immediately.

Ingredients
4 chicken breasts, boneless & skinless
2 tbsp olive oil
¾ tsp salt
½ tsp dried oregano
Fresh cracked pepper

For the dressing
⅓ cup olive oil
¼ cup fresh squeezed lemon juice
½ tsp dried oregano
½ tsp salt

BBQ Maintenance
To keep your grates clean, don't turn off the gas once you have removed your barbecued meat. Keep the heat on and the lid closed for 10 minutes. Then go back and clean the grates. It is easier to remove any bits stuck to your BBQ when the grates are hot. Plus, your BBQ is clean the next time you go out to use it!

Grill (450ºF 220ºC) Serves (4) Time to Table (30 min) Diet (gf)

food is love

3 greek sisters

CHICKEN & LEEK PIE FILLING

Kotopita (Ko-TOH-pee-tah)

The convenience of ready roasted chickens in grocery stores makes this dish a cinch to put together. Our family in Greece did not often use mushrooms, but over the years they have become increasingly popular. Mushrooms add great flavour to the dish. We have used both button and cremini, but Portobello mushrooms can also be used.

1   Consider your phyllo pie of choice. Prepare homemade phyllo, or thaw prepared phyllo and set aside.

2   To make filling, remove the skin from the roasting chicken and discard. Remove the meat from the bones and chop into small pieces. Transfer to a large bowl and season with oregano and fresh cracked pepper. Set aside.

3   Heat the olive oil and butter in a large saucepan over medium-high heat. Add the mushrooms, thyme and a pinch of salt. Once the mushrooms start to release liquid, add the wine. Reduce the heat to medium and cook until all of the liquid has evaporated. Remove from heat and transfer to the bowl with the chicken.

4   Heat the olive oil in the same saucepan over medium heat. Add the shallot, leeks and pinch of salt. Cook until the shallots and leeks are soft, about 5 minutes. Remove from heat and transfer to the bowl with the chicken. Set aside to cool.

5   Add the crumbled feta cheese to the cooled filling and mix.

Your filling is now complete and ready to be added to a phyllo pastry of your choice.

To place this filling in a homemade phyllo pie refer to page 229 for preparation and cooking instructions.

To place this filling in a homemade spiral pie refer to page 233 for preparation and cooking instructions.

To place this filling in a prepared phyllo pastry refer to page 237 for preparation and cooking instructions.

Ingredients
1 phyllo pie of choice, page 229, 233 or 237
1 roasting chicken, cooked
1 tsp dried oregano
Fresh cracked pepper
2 tbsp olive oil
2 tbsp butter
5 cups white button and cremini mushrooms, quartered
Fresh thyme, chopped
Pinch of salt
¼ cup white wine
2 tbsp olive oil
1 shallot, minced
2 leeks, white and pale green parts, thinly sliced
Pinch of salt
1 cup feta cheese, crumbled

Make Ahead
This filling can be prepared and stored in the refrigerator up to 1 day in advance.

Serves 6-8   Time to Table for filling   30 min

food is love

And another child's world is changed forever.

After an entire day making noodles with our maternal grandparents,
our grandmother asked us if we could prepare liver for dinner while
she lay down for a nap. We were young teens at the time and said
yes. We went to the kitchen, and quickly recalled there was no
fridge. Next to a picturesque blue window hung a lamb,
slaughtered early that morning. The liver was still inside the lamb.
We were changed forever.

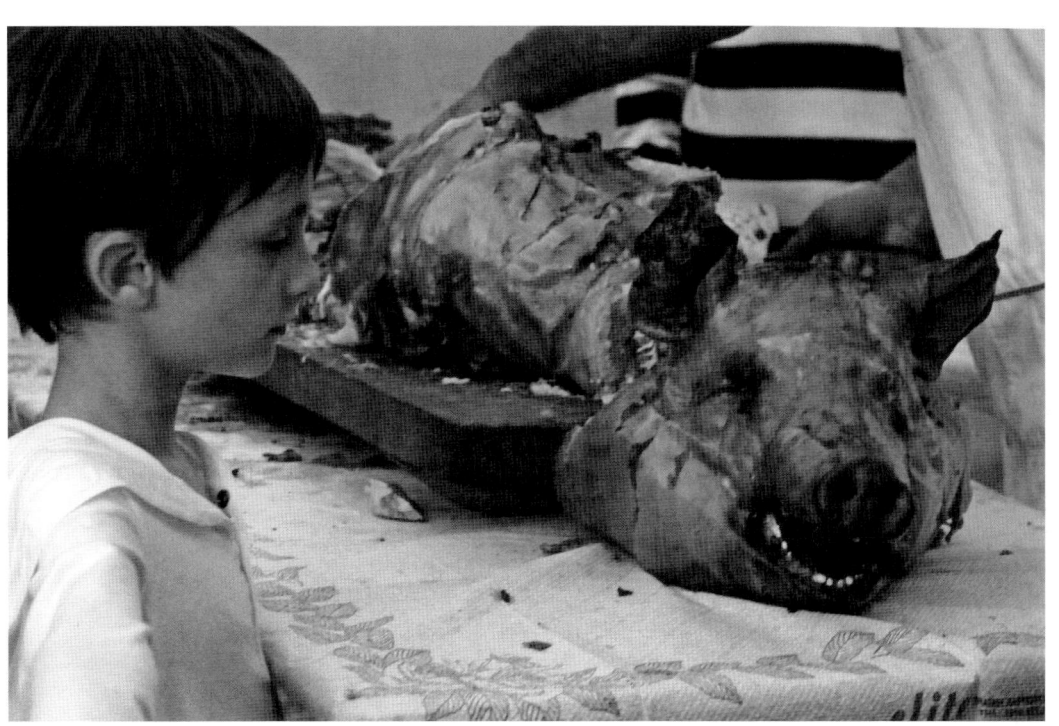

3 greek sisters

FENNEL RIBS

Paidakia Me Sporous Maratho (Pah-ee-DAH-kee-ah Me SPO-rous MAH-rah-tho)

When our mom made these ribs growing up, it immediately felt like a special day. We could never really figure out what made these ribs so much tastier than ribs we had anywhere else. We now know the secret: fennel seeds. This one simple ingredient puts these ribs into a league of their own.

1. In a small saucepan, whisk the tomato paste and olive oil until combined. Continue whisking and add the water. Whisk in the remaining sauce ingredients, and place on stovetop over high heat. Bring to a boil, then reduce heat and simmer for 5 minutes. Remove from the heat and set aside to cool.

2. Arrange the lemon slices along the bottom of a large roasting pan with a fitted lid and set aside. Remove the thin membrane along the backside of the ribs, see below.

3. Place the ribs in the roasting pan. If ribs do not lie flat, cut the ribs into smaller sections. Liberally salt the ribs on both sides. Coat the ribs with about one-third of the sauce.

4. Carefully pour the water into the roasting pan around the ribs, ensuring that you do not pour the water on top of the ribs and remove the sauce.

5. Place the roasting pan, covered, in the middle of a preheated oven for 2-2½ hours, or until the rib meat is extremely tender and literally falls off the bone.

6. Carefully remove the ribs from roasting pan and arrange on a baking sheet. Cut into individual ribs or into smaller serving pieces and coat generously with the remaining sauce. Place in the middle of a preheated oven and broil for about 3 minutes per side. Serve.

Removing Membrane from Ribs
To remove the thin membrane along the backside of the ribs, insert a sharp knife underneath the membrane so that you can grab the membrane with your fingers. (Using a paper towel to hold the membrane helps to pull the membrane off easily.) Grab the membrane tightly and pull back. You should be able to pull the entire membrane off. If not, repeat and pull again until the entire membrane has been removed.

Ingredients
For the Sauce
5 tbsp tomato paste
6 tbsp olive oil
6 tbsp water
4 garlic cloves, minced
½ cup brown sugar
3 tbsp balsamic vinegar
3 tbsp fresh squeezed lemon juice
2 tbsp fennel seeds
2 tbsp honey
2½ tsp sweet paprika
2 tsp salt
1½ tsp cayenne pepper
1 tsp dried oregano

For the Ribs
1 lemon, sliced
2 racks baby back ribs
Salt
½ cup water

In a Pinch?
Add fennel seeds to your favourite BBQ sauce to prepare this recipe.

Bake 300°F / 150°C Serves 4 Time to Table 3 hours Diet gf

food is love

KREATOPITA PIE FILLING

(Kreh-ah-TOH-pee-tah)

Meat pies are prevalent in all parts of Greece. This recipe comes from Macedonia, birthplace of Alexander the Great and Aristotle. Many years ago, a cousin of ours married a handsome man from Macedonia, and it wasn't long before she quickly learned new and wonderful dishes that she relished bringing to family get-togethers. This one quickly became her signature dish. Rather than using ground pork, a pork tenderloin is flavoured with onions, red peppers, and allspice until the medley is sweet and flavourful.

Ingredients
1 phyllo pie of choice, page 229, 233 or 237
1 pork tenderloin, 1 lb (500 g), silverskin removed
Olive oil for coating
Coarse salt
Dried oregano
Fresh cracked pepper
¼ cup olive oil
4 yellow onions, thinly sliced
4 red bell peppers, thinly sliced
2 hot banana peppers, thinly sliced
4 garlic cloves, minced
½ tsp salt
¼ tsp dried red chilies
3 tbsp tomato paste
¼ cup hot water
1 tsp dried oregano
¾ tsp ground allspice
Fresh cracked pepper

In the Oven
If you don't have a barbecue, the tenderloin can be seared in a skillet for 2-3 minutes on each side and placed in a 300°F (150°C) oven for 45 minutes or until a thermometer registers 170°F (77°C).

1 Consider your phyllo pie of choice. Prepare homemade phyllo, or thaw prepared phyllo and set aside.

2 For the filling, trim away the excess fat and silver skin from the tenderloin. Coat the tenderloin with olive oil, and season liberally with coarse salt, oregano and pepper.

3 Place the tenderloin on a preheated grill and sear about 2-3 minutes per side. Arrange the tenderloin on one half of the grill and turn the heat on that side of the grill off. Cook the tenderloin over this indirect heat, with the lid closed, for 20 minutes.

4 Transfer the tenderloin to a cutting board, cover with aluminum foil and set aside to rest for 10 minutes.

5 Use two forks to pull or shred the pork apart. Place the pulled pork in a large bowl and set aside.

6 Heat the olive oil in a wide saucepan, over medium-high heat. Add the onions and peppers and sauté until soft, about 10 minutes. Add the garlic, salt, and chilies and continue cooking for a minute further. In a separate small bowl, dilute the tomato paste in the hot water and add to the saucepan. Add the remaining ingredients and stir.

7 Remove the saucepan from the heat and add the ingredients to the bowl with the pulled pork. Gently mix ingredients together and set aside to cool completely.

Your filling is now complete and ready to be added to a phyllo pastry of your choice. *Continued on next page.*

3 greek sisters

Grill (350°F 180°C) Serves (6-8) Time to Table for filling (1 hour)

To place this filling in a homemade phyllo pie refer to page 229 for preparation and cooking instructions.

To place this filling in a homemade spiral pie refer to page 233 for preparation and cooking instructions.

To place this filling in a prepared phyllo pastry refer to page 237 for preparation and cooking instructions.

Make Ahead
This filling can be prepared
and stored in the refrigerator
up to 1 day in advance.

food is love

3 greek sisters

SOFRITO

(Soh-FREE-toh)

Sofrito is a specialty on the beautiful island of Corfu, (Kerkyra), located on the Ionian coast of Greece, facing Italy. Influences of Venetian rule are evident throughout the island's architecture and cuisine.
In Italian, sofrito means to slowly fry. In this dish, veal is slowly fried while ingredients such as onion, garlic and wine are added. The result is fragrant and mouthwatering. Pork scallopini can be used in place of veal if preferred.

1. Lightly season each side of the veal scaloppini with salt and pepper. Coat with flour and shake off any excess.

2. In a large sauté pan heat 3 tablespoons of the olive oil over medium-high heat. Add a single layer of veal and cook until browned on both sides, about 1-2 minutes per side. Cook in batches to avoid over-crowding. Transfer veal to a dish.

3. In the same sauté pan add the remaining olive oil, onion and garlic and sauté for two minutes.

4. Increase the heat to high and add the wine. Cook until the wine has reduced by half, scraping any brown bits from the bottom of the pan with a wooden spoon.

5. Return the veal to the pan, add the stock and bring to a boil. Reduce the heat to medium-low and maintain a low-boil until the meat is soft and the sauce has reduced and thickened, about 45-minutes to 1-hour.

6. Remove the pan from the heat and stir in the fresh parsley. Serve.

Ingredients
1 lb (500 g) veal scallopini
Salt & Pepper
¼ cup all-purpose flour
5 tbsp olive oil
1 yellow onion, thinly sliced
3 garlic cloves, minced
½ cup white wine
1½ cups beef stock
⅔ cup fresh parsley, chopped

Substitution
If using pork, use boneless pork loin chops and pound till they are ¼-inch (6 mm) thick.

Serves 4   Time to Table 1 ¼ hours   Diet gf

food is love

3 greek sisters

SPETZOFAI

(Speh-tzoh-FAH-ee)

A variety of bell and hot peppers are sautéed with sausages in this rustic dish - a specialty found in Northern Greece. The peppers and onions are slowly cooked until soft and sweet and then simmered with tomatoes and Greek sausage. They can be enjoyed with bread or a side of mashed or fried potatoes.

1 Slice the sausage into 1-inch (2.5 cm) rounds.

2 Heat the olive oil in a large saucepan over medium-high heat. Add the sausage to the hot oil and cook until browned on all sides. Transfer sausages to a bowl and set aside. If necessary, drain the pan of any excess fat.

3 Add the sliced peppers, onions and salt to the same saucepan and sauté over medium heat until softened, about 10 minutes (if pan is too dry, add another 2 tablespoons of olive oil). Add the garlic and sauté for a minute further. Add the wine and reduce by half. Add the tomatoes, tomato paste and oregano and sauté until the tomatoes begin to boil and break down.

4 Return the browned sausages to the pan and submerge the sausages in the liquid. Stirring occasionally, maintain a low-boil and cook until sauce reduces slightly, about 20 minutes.

5 Season with fresh cracked pepper to taste and serve.

Ingredients
4 Greek sausages
2 tbsp olive oil
3 bell peppers (red, yellow & orange), seeds removed, thinly sliced
1 hot banana pepper, seeds removed, thinly sliced
2 yellow onions, thinly sliced
½ tsp salt
4 garlic cloves, roughly chopped
½ cup dry white wine
3 vine-ripened tomatoes, diced
1 tbsp tomato paste
1 tsp dried oregano
Fresh cracked pepper

Variation
Greek sausages can be substituted with any kind of spicy or bold flavoured sausage.

Leftover Tomato Paste
Unused tomato paste can be kept in the refrigerator covered with oil for 7 days or in freezer for 6 months.

Homemade Sausages
Head to page 239 for a recipe on how to make your very own homemade sausages.

food is love

Serves (4) Time to Table (45 min) Diet (gf)

3 greek sisters

LAMB FRICASSEE WITH DILL & GREENS

Arni Fricassee (Ahr-NEE Free-kah-SEH)

Lamb fricassee is a stew of lamb chops, greens and dill, finished with a refreshing and creamy Avgolemono sauce. No water is needed for this stew, as the greens will release all the liquid that is required for cooking. We love this dish because it really represents how Greeks love to eat: a bit of meat, lots of greens, and a lemony finish. Serve with plenty of bread.

Ingredients
8 lamb chops (use a variety: rib, loin, shoulder)
2 tbsp olive oil
1 yellow onion, diced
8 scallions, both white & green parts, chopped
¼ cup fresh dill, chopped
1 cup white wine
1 tsp salt
1¼ cups water
Fresh cracked pepper
1 bunch spinach, washed & coarsely chopped
2 bunches green leaf lettuce, washed & coarsely chopped

For the Avgolemono Sauce
1 cup cooking liquid
Juice of 1½ lemons
2 eggs, separated

1. Trim the fat from the lamb chops.

2. In a large Dutch oven, heat the olive oil over high heat. Brown the lamb and transfer to a plate. If necessary, brown the lamb in batches to avoid over-crowding.

3. Reduce heat to medium and add the yellow onions to the pot. Cook until soft, about 5 minutes.

4. Return the lamb to the pot along with any juices. Add the scallions, dill, wine, water, salt and pepper. Bring ingredients to a boil, then reduce heat and simmer, covered, for 45 minutes.

5. Add the spinach and lettuce to the pot a handful at a time, until they have wilted and reduced in volume. Simmer, partially covered, for 30 minutes or until the liquid has reduced and the lamb is soft.

6. For the Avgolemono sauce, carefully remove 1 cup of the hot cooking liquid from the pot. Stir in the lemon juice and set aside. Add the egg whites to the bowl of a stand-mixer fitted with a whisk attachment. Beat the whites on high-speed until soft peaks form. With the mixer running add the egg yolks and slowly add the cup of hot liquid and lemon juice. Ensure that the liquid is added slowly so that the eggs do not curdle. Adding hot liquid slowly to eggs is referred to as tempering.

7. Return the Avgolemono sauce to the pot with lamb and greens. Serve immediately.

Serves 4 | Time to Table 2 hours | Diet gf

food is love

Make Ahead
The lamb mixture can be prepared and refrigerated for up to 1 day in advance. Bring to room temperature before shaping into patties and grilling.

3 greek sisters

LAMB BURGERS

Keftedes Me Arni (Keh-FTEH-des Meh Ahr-NEE)

Lamb burgers are a crowd pleaser and make for perfect sliders when entertaining. The ground lamb is seasoned with fresh herbs and spices and then grilled to perfection. You are sure to get many compliments when serving these up to guests.

1 Place all of the ingredients in a large bowl. Use your hands to thoroughly mix ingredients together. Shape lamb mixture into 4 patties.

2 Place the patties on a preheated grill and cook for 4-6 minutes on each side. Do not overcook or the patties will become dry.

3 Serve on a sesame seed bun topped with feta cheese, red onions or our Cherry Tomato Relish recipe below.

Gluten-Friendly
Use gluten-free breadcrumbs to make this recipe completely gluten-free.

Coridander Seeds
Whole coriander seeds can be ground using a mortar and pestle for a superior and more pronounced flavour in the lamb burgers.

Make Ahead
Cherry Tomato relish can be stored in an airtight container and refrigerated for up to 1 week in advance.

Cherry Tomato Relish

Heat the oil in a small saucepan over medium heat. Add the shallots and garlic and sauté for 2-3 minutes. Add the chili flakes and sauté for 1 minute further.

Add the tomatoes and sauté until the tomatoes begin to break down, about 3 minutes. Add the remaining ingredients, except for the basil. Bring to a boil and continue boiling until liquid has reduced and thickened, about 20 minutes. Remove from the heat and set aside to cool completely.

Add the basil, mix and transfer to a jar with a fitted lid. Store in the refrigerator until ready to serve.

Makes (2 cups)   Time to Table (30 min)

Ingredients
1 lb (500 g) ground lamb
½ cup fresh parsley, minced
¼ cup fresh chives, minced
¼ cup fresh dill, minced
2 tbsp ground cumin
1 tbsp ground coriander seed
1 tbsp sweet paprika
½ tsp cayenne pepper
2 garlic cloves, minced
1 egg
⅓ cup breadcrumbs
½ tsp salt
Fresh cracked pepper

Cherry Tomato Relish
2 tbsp olive oil
3 shallots, minced
3 garlic cloves, minced
¼ tsp dried red chilies
2 cups cherry tomatoes, halved
½ cup sun-dried tomatoes, chopped
½ cup Kalamata olives, pitted, halved
2 tbsp capers, drained
¼ tsp salt
1 tsp sugar
1 cup water
2 tbsp fresh basil, chopped

Grill (med) Serves (4) Time to Table (25 min)

food is love

3 greek sisters

LAMB CHOPS WITH BRANDY MINT SAUCE

Paidakia (Pah-ee-DAH-kee-ah)

A quick appetizer that is sure to impress. Lamb chops are formally dressed with a simple yet elegant sauce of brandy and mint.

1. Add the shallot, brandy and mint to a small saucepan over high heat. Bring to a boil and continue boiling until 1-2 tablespoons of liquid is left, about 5 minutes. Set aside to cool.

2. Trim the fat from the loin chops. Coat the chops with the minced garlic. Liberally salt and pepper both sides of the chops and lightly coat with olive oil.

3. Heat a large ovenproof skillet over high heat. Add the loin chops to the hot skillet and sear for 2 minutes. Flip the chops and sear for a minute further.

4. Place the pan in the middle of a preheated oven for 5-8 minutes for medium lamb chops. Remove from oven, tent with aluminum foil and set aside for 5 minutes.

5. Meanwhile, add the mint, the mayonnaise and salt to the saucepan set aside earlier and mix.

6. Arrange the lamb chops on a serving platter and top with the brandy-mint sauce. Serve immediately.

Searing Meat
To sear meat well, your skillet needs to be piping hot. Add a few drops of water to the skillet, if the water sizzles and evaporates, your skillet is ready.

Ingredients
For the Sauce
1 shallot, minced
⅓ cup Metaxa, or other brandy
½ cup fresh mint, chopped
⅓ cup mayonnaise
Pinch of salt

For the Lamb Chops
8 lamb loin chops, about ¾ to 1-inch (2.5 cm) thick
2 garlic cloves, minced
Salt
Fresh cracked pepper
Olive oil for coating

Bake (450°F 230°C) Serves (4) Time to Table (30 min) Diet (gf)

food is love

3 greek sisters

LAMB SHANKS

Bouti Arni (BOO-tee Ahr-NEE)

Fancy ingredients are not required to make delectable lamb shanks, you need only patience. The meat will fall off the bone if cooked at a low temperature for a couple of hours. The lamb is cooked in garlic and wine and then finished off with lemon and mint. It smells and tastes divine. So simple and so good.

1. Trim the fat from the lamb shanks. Using a sharp knife, cut ½-inch (12 mm) deep slits into the meaty side of the lamb and insert the sliced garlic into each slit.

2. Heat the olive oil in a large pot over high heat. Brown the lamb on all sides, about 2-3 minutes per side. Remove the lamb from the heat and transfer to a cutting board.

3. Coat the lamb with the crushed garlic. Season liberally with oregano, salt, and pepper.

4. Return the lamb to the pot and add the wine over high heat. Bring the wine to a boil.

5. Promptly remove the pot from the heat and place in the middle of a preheated oven, covered, for 2 hours, turning the lamb shanks halfway through the cooking time.

6. The lamb meat should be fall-off-the-bone tender. Transfer the lamb shanks to a serving platter. Squeeze with lemon juice and top with fresh mint. Serve.

Ingredients
4 lamb shanks
12 garlic cloves, 6 sliced & 6 crushed
3 tbsp olive oil
Dried oregano
Salt
Fresh cracked pepper
¾ cup red wine
Juice of ½ lemon
2 tbsp fresh mint, chopped

food is love

Bake 300°F / 150°C | Serves 4 | Time to Table 2½ hours | Diet gf

KLEFTIKO

(KLEH-ftee-koh)

During the Revolution in the hillsides of Greece, rebels would steal a lamb or a goat and cook it in the ground in a stone-oven covered with mud for several hours. Hiding the meat in the ground would ensure that no steam would escape. The Kleftiko, or "stolen meat" would later fill the bellies of the rebels, without having given their location away. Today, Kleftiko is made with parchment paper, in the same way that the French would prepare a piece of meat "en papillote". This dish is as succulent as the days of the Revolution. Its aroma will sound an alarm notifying your household that something very delicious is waiting in the kitchen.

Ingredients

1 lamb shoulder, 3 lb (1½ kg), bone-in
4 garlic cloves, slivered
Salt
2 tbsp olive oil
Juice of 1 lemon
1 tsp dried oregano
Fresh cracked pepper
Drizzle of olive oil

Make Ahead

If the edges of the parchment paper do not come together easily for you, then use butcher's twine to tie it together into a bundle.

1. Use a sharp knife to remove any excess fat from the lamb.

2. Cut ½-inch (12 mm) deep slits into the meaty side of the lamb and insert slivers of garlic into each slit. Liberally season the lamb with salt on all sides.

3. Heat the olive oil in a large pan over high heat. Brown the lamb on all sides, about 3-4 minutes per side. Remove the lamb from pan and drain on paper towels. *Continued on next page.*

3 greek sisters

Bake 350°F 180°C | Serves 4 | Time to Table 2 hours | Diet gf

4 Cut two 1-metre long pieces of parchment paper. Lay one sheet of parchment paper on a flat work surface. Place the lamb in the centre of the parchment paper. Squeeze the lemon juice over the entire surface of the lamb. Season the lamb with oregano, pepper and a drizzle of olive oil. Place the second sheet of parchment on top of the lamb. Grab the edges of the parchment paper together. Tuck and fold them upwards. Continue folding the parchment and ensure that all of the lamb is sealed in, with no chance of steam escaping while it is cooking.

5 Transfer the lamb bundle to a roasting pan. Place in the middle of a preheated oven for 1½ hours.

6 Carefully open the the parchment paper and serve immediately.

food is love

How to Boil Perfect Hard-Boiled Eggs

Choose eggs that have been in the refrigerator for about 3 days as these eggs will be easier to peel than fresh eggs. Place in a pot in a single layer. Fill pot with enough cold water to just cover the eggs. Bring to a boil over high heat. Immediately remove pot from the heat and set aside covered, for 20 minutes. Drain and rinse eggs with cold water. Peel. Eggs are now ready for use.

3 greek sisters

MEATLOAF

Rolo Kima Me Avga (ROH-loh Kee-MAH Meh Ahv-GAH)

Meatloaf feels very retro to us, especially this Greek meatloaf recipe with eggs. We ate this often as children, but not so much as we got older, it must have fallen out of favour with our mom. Now we serve it up to our own kids, and like us, they love the hidden eggs inside the loaf as much as we did.
The meat can be prepared quickly the night before, making this meal an easy weeknight solution.

1. Heat the olive oil in a large skillet over medium heat. Add the onion and sauté until softened, about 5 minutes. Add the garlic and sauté a minute further. Transfer to a large bowl.

2. Add the remaining ingredients to the large bowl and mix thoroughly with your hands. Set aside to rest in the refrigerator for 1 hour or up to 1 day in advance.

3. Arrange half of the mixture on a lightly greased rimmed baking sheet. Shape into a log about 8-inches (20 cm) long. Firmly press the mixture along the centre to create a trough. Line up the hard-boiled eggs in the trough, bottom to tip. Cover the eggs with the remaining meat mixture. Press the mixture firmly along the sides to completely encase the eggs and to seal the sides. Pat gently until you have a loaf. Place in the middle of a preheated oven for 1¼ hours.

4. Drain the fat and set meatloaf aside for 5 minutes before removing from the pan.

5. Meanwhile prepare the Lemon Dressing. Add the ingredients to a small bowl and whisk.

6. Transfer meatloaf to a cutting board and use a serrated knife to cut into thick slices. Arrange on a platter and drizzle with Lemon Dressing. Serve.

Ingredients
2 tbsp olive oil
1 yellow onion, minced
3 garlic cloves, minced
1½ lb (750 g) ground beef
1 egg
2 tbsp white wine
½ cup breadcrumbs
1 tsp Dijon mustard
½ cup feta cheese, crumbled
¼ cup fresh parsley, chopped
¼ cup fresh mint, chopped
1 tsp dried oregano
1½ tsp salt
Fresh cracked pepper
Olive oil for greasing
4 eggs, hard-boiled

For the Lemon Dressing
¼ cup olive oil
2 tbsp fresh squeezed lemon juice
½ tsp dried oregano
¼ tsp salt

Rimmed Baking Sheet
Be sure to use a rimmed baking sheet when preparing this recipe as the loaf will release fatty oils during cooking. These oils will end up in your oven and can be potentially hazardous.

Gluten Friendly
Use gluten-free breadcrumbs to make this recipe completely gluten-free.

food is love

| Bake | 350°F 180°C | Serves | 6 | Time to Table | 2¾ hours |

3 greek sisters

SOUTZOUKAKIA

(Sou-dzou-KAH-kee-ah)

Travel to Greece, visit a taverna, and you are likely to find these delectable meatballs on the menu. The inspiration for these meatballs comes from Smyrna, (modern day Izmir, Turkey). These oblong-shaped meatballs are made with cumin and cinnamon, and then simmered in a tasty red tomato sauce. They can be served over a bed of rice, skinny fries, or mashed potatoes.

1. For the meatballs, process the bread slices in a food processor until you have a fine crumb. Transfer to a medium-sized bowl and add the remaining ingredients. Mix thoroughly with your hands. Cover and place in refrigerator for at least an hour, or overnight.

2. Shape meat mixture into oblong meatballs about 2-inches (5 cm) long and place on a lightly greased baking sheet. Place in the middle of a preheated oven for 20 minutes until golden brown and almost cooked through.

3. Meanwhile, prepare the tomato sauce. In a blender or food processor add the canned tomatoes and process until smooth. Set aside.

4. Heat the olive oil in a wide-bottomed saucepan over medium heat. Add the onion and sauté until soft, about 5 minutes. Add the garlic and sauté for a minute further. Add the tomato purée and the remaining ingredients, stir and bring to a boil. Lower heat and simmer for 20 minutes.

5. Add the cooked meatballs to the tomato sauce and simmer for an additional 15 minutes. Serve warm.

Make Ahead
The sauce can be made up to 2 days in advance. Gently reheat before adding the meatballs and simmering. The meatballs can be cooked a day in advance before adding to the tomato sauce.

Gluten Friendly
Use gluten-free breadcrumbs to make this recipe completely gluten-free.

Ingredients
For the Meatballs
2 slices whole-wheat bread
1 lb (500 g) ground beef, extra lean
1 yellow onion, minced
3 garlic cloves, minced
1 egg
¼ cup fresh parsley, chopped
2 tbsp white wine
1 tsp ground cumin
1 tsp dried oregano
1 tsp salt
½ tsp ground cinnamon
Fresh cracked pepper

For the Sauce
1 can (28 oz/796 mL) plum tomatoes
2 tbsp olive oil
1 yellow onion, minced
2 garlic cloves, minced
1 tbsp dried oregano
1 bay leaf
1 tsp salt
¾ tsp ground cumin
Fresh cracked pepper

food is love

Bake (450°F / 230°C) Makes (20-22) Time to Table (2¼ hours)

3 greek sisters

BEEF BARLEY & OLIVE STEW

Stifado Me Elies (Stee-FA-do Meh Eh-LEE-ehs)

Olives, olives, olives! Yes, we cannot get enough of them. This dish uses lots of olives, onions and peppers for a hearty beef stew. The addition of barley makes it a complete meal.

1 Coat the stewing beef with salt and flour. Set aside.

2 In a large Dutch oven, heat the olive oil over high heat. Brown the beef and transfer to a plate. If necessary, brown the beef in batches to avoid over-crowding.

3 Reduce heat to medium and add the onions and peppers to the pot. Sprinkle with salt and sauté until soft, about 5 minutes. Add the garlic and sauté for a minute further.

4 Return the browned beef to pot over high heat. Add the bay leaf and wine and cook until the wine has reduced by half. Add the tomato paste, beef broth, oregano and fresh cracked pepper and stir. Bring to a boil, remove from the stovetop and place in the middle of a preheated oven, covered, for 1 hour.

5 Add the olives and barley to the pot, stir and continue cooking in the oven, covered for 45 minutes, or until the barley is cooked. Discard bay leaf and serve hot.

Ingredients
1 lb (500 g) stewing beef, cubed
½ tsp salt
2 tbsp all-purpose flour
¼ cup olive oil
1 large yellow onion, thinly sliced
3 bell peppers, (red, yellow, or orange) thinly sliced
½ tsp salt
5 garlic cloves, roughly chopped
1 bay leaf
1 cup full-bodied red wine
2 tbsp tomato paste
3 cups beef broth
½ tsp dried oregano
Fresh cracked pepper
½ cup green olives, pitted & roughly chopped
½ cup black olives, pitted & roughly chopped
⅔ cup pot barley

Make Ahead
Stew can be stored in an airtight container and frozen for up to 3 months.

No oven required
You can reduce the heat to low and continue cooking this entire meal on your stovetop.

Substitution
This stew can be enjoyed with lamb or venison cubes.

Bake 350°F 180°C Serves 4 Time to Table 2 ½ hours

food is love

STUFFED CABBAGE ROLLS WITH A LEMON FINISH

Lahanodolmades Me Avgolemono (Lah-hah-no-dohl-MAH-des Meh Ahv-goh-LEH-moh-noh)

Cabbage rolls make a hearty, comforting meal. The filling consists of ground beef, rice and sauerkraut, the latter being an ingredient found in Northern Greek cooking. Cabbage rolls can be cooked in a tomato sauce but we prefer the lemon sauce, Avgolemono, that is popular throughout Greece. Avgolemono is a beautiful, refreshing finish to this dish and is unique to the Greek kitchen.

Ingredients

1 lb (500 g) extra-lean ground beef
¼ cup olive oil
2 yellow onions, minced
Pinch of salt
3 garlic cloves, minced
1 egg
1 cup sauerkraut
1 tbsp tomato paste
½ cup Arborio rice, rinsed
1 tsp salt
½ cup fresh parsley, minced
1 tbsp dried oregano
Fresh cracked pepper
5 cups water
1 tsp salt
1 large, or 2 medium heads
Savoy cabbage
¼ cup olive oil
Fresh cracked pepper

For the Avgolemono
1 cup cooking liquid
Juice of 1½ lemons
2 eggs, separated

Beef

We highly recommend using extra-lean ground beef for this dish as the fat cannot be drained away.

1. Place the ground beef in a large bowl and set aside.

2. Add the olive oil, onions and salt to a medium sauté pan and cook over medium heat until soft and translucent, about 5 minutes. Add the garlic and cook for a minute further. Remove from the heat and transfer to the bowl with the beef. Set aside to cool.

3. Add the remaining ingredients up until the water to the bowl and use your hands to mix thoroughly. Set aside.

4. Add the 5 cups water and 1 teaspoon salt to a large pot and bring to a boil. Meanwhile, trim the bottom of the cabbage with a sharp knife. Peel away the cabbage leaves and rinse them under cold water. Continue peeling the leaves back and trimming the cabbage core until all of the cabbage leaves have been separated and rinsed.

5. Place the cabbage leaves in the pot of boiling water and blanch until the leaves have softened, about 5-8 minutes. Reserve the cabbage water.

6. Line the bottom of a Dutch oven with 2-3 of the largest outer cabbage leaves. These leaves will prevent the rolls from sticking to the bottom of the pot. Reserve 2-3 leaves to cover the completed rolls.

7. Pare off any coarse veins from the cabbage leaves. On a flat surface, place the largest cabbage leaf, vein side down. *Continued on next page.*

3 greek sisters

Bake (350°F / 180°C) Serves (6-8) Time to Table (3 hours)

Add 2 heaping tablespoons of the filling at the end of the leaf closest to you.

8   Roll the leaf over the filling, tuck the sides in, and continue rolling. (Do not fold the roll too tightly, as the rice will need room to expand.) Place the cabbage roll in the pot. Continue this process with the remaining leaves, ensuring that the filling size is adjusted according to the size of the leaf. Cover the top of the completed cabbage rolls with the reserved leaves that were set aside earlier to help prevent the rolls from scorching.

9   Completely cover the cabbage rolls with 4 cups of the reserved cabbage water. Bring liquid to a boil, remove from the heat and cover with a fitted lid. Place in the middle of a preheated oven for 1½ hours. Remove from the oven and discard the top leaves.

10   For the Avgolemono sauce, carefully remove 1 cup of the hot cooking liquid from the pot. Stir in the lemon juice and set aside. Add the egg whites to the bowl of a stand-mixer fitted with a whisk attachment. Beat the whites on high-speed until soft peaks form. With the mixer running add the egg yolks and slowly add the cup of hot liquid and lemon juice. Ensure that the liquid is added slowly so that the eggs do not curdle. Adding hot liquid slowly to eggs is referred to as tempering.

11   Return the Avgolemono sauce to the pot with the cooked cabbage rolls. Hold the pot with both hands and slowly tilt it back and forth to allow the Avgolemono sauce to reach all of the cabbage rolls. Carefully serve the rolls and top each roll with some Avgolemono sauce.

Freezing
Cabbage rolls can be stored in the freezer for up to one month as long as Avgolemono sauce has not been added. Before serving, thaw rolls, reheat using stovetop, and prepare Avgolemono sauce.

No oven required
You can reduce the heat to low and continue cooking this entire meal on your stovetop.

food is love

I fought hard to have
Smelts, one of my
favourite seaside meals,
in this cookbook!
-Eleni

3 greek sisters

SMELTS

Marithes (Mah-REE-thes)

These popular little fish are so small that the entire fish is eaten, although we prefer to leave the tails on the plates, just to keep score. Like french fries, they are eaten with your fingers while piping hot. They are enjoyed alongside other dips and appetizers, while sipping chilled ouzo. If you are not sitting by the ocean while eating these little marithes, you will have to close your eyes and imagine the sounds of the Mediterranean sea hitting the shore. Anchovies or whiting can also be prepared this way.

Ingredients
1 lb (500 g) smelts
Salt & pepper
All-purpose flour for dredging
Vegetable oil for frying
Lemon wedges

1. Rinse the smelts under cold water.

2. Liberally season the smelts with salt and pepper.

3. Just before frying, dredge the smelts with flour. Shake off any excess flour.

4. Fill a deep frying pan with enough oil to reach a depth of 3-inches (7.5 cm). Heat the oil over high heat, or until a thermometer registers 375°F (190°C). Add the fish to the hot oil and cook until golden brown, about 3-4 minutes. Do not overcrowd, cook in batches if necessary. Drain the fried fish on a paper towel to absorb any excess oil.

5. Squeeze the lemon juice on the fish just before you are ready to pop them in your mouth. Serve piping hot.

Size of the Smelts
The smaller the fish, the better. When the fish are small the bones are also soft and easier to eat whole. If the fish are big, longer than 4-inches (10 cm), then you will have to remove the head and bones before frying.

Gutting Larger Smelts (4-inches (10 cm) or longer)
With a sharp knife, make an incision on the underside of the fish, between the head and tail, and squeeze out the insides. Rinse and pat dry with a paper towel.

Tip
Dredge the fish with flour only a few minutes before you are ready to fry, otherwise the flour will absorb moisture and become gummy.

Serves (4) Time to Table (30 min) Diet (v)

food is love

3 greek sisters

COD BURGERS

Psarokeftedes (Psah-roh-keh-FTEH-des)

Cod is a fish commonly eaten in Greece. Before the average home had a refrigerator, cod was sold as "Bakaliaros," a large, flat, hard, dried and heavily salted whole fish. It had to be immersed in water for days to draw out the excess salt before it could be used for cooking. Cod can still be found prepared in this way at many grocery stores and if you are feeling nostalgic, give it a go.

Fresh or frozen cod will work nicely when making these little cakes. They are mild in flavour and easy to make. The patty holds its shape well, making it ideal to cook in the oven, rather than deep-frying. These patties taste great all on their own, however, they can be dressed up as a burger too, with simple toppings such as: tomatoes, lettuce, or even our Saffron Dipping Sauce on page 63.

1. Place the potatoes in a small pot, cover with water and bring to boil. Continue boiling for 10 minutes. Remove from the heat and drain. Transfer to a large bowl and mash the potato.

2. Finely chop the cod and place in a colander. Squeeze the fish to remove any excess water. Add to the bowl with the mashed potato.

3. Add the remaining ingredients to the bowl and use your hands to mix the ingredients thoroughly. Shape into 10 burger patties and place on a well-greased baking sheet. Place in the middle of a preheated oven for 20-25 minutes or until lightly golden brown.

4. Serve fish burgers on a bun with your favourite toppings.

Ingredients
- 2 yellow potatoes, ½ lb (250g), peeled, cubed
- 1 lb (500 g) cod
- 10 cherry tomatoes, quartered
- 5 scallions, white & pale green parts, chopped
- 2 shallots, minced
- 2 garlic cloves, minced
- ½ cup breadcrumbs
- 2 tbsp fresh parsley, minced
- 1 tbsp fresh dill, minced
- 2 tbsp olive oil
- 1 tbsp Dijon mustard
- 1 egg
- Juice of ½ lemon
- 1 tsp salt
- Fresh cracked pepper
- Olive oil for greasing

Gluten Friendly
Use gluten-free breadcrumbs to make this recipe completely gluten-free.

Substitutions
Cod can be substituted with any lean, firm white fish such as haddock, halibut or sea bass.

food is love

| Bake | 425°F 220°C | Makes | 10 | Time to Table | 45 min | Diet | v |

BAKED FISH CASSEROLE

Psari Sto Fourno (PSAH-ree Sto FOUR-no)

Some of our favourite meals are the simplest. This casserole uses a firm white fish and staple vegetables, so it makes for an easy mid-week meal, but we bet you'll want to make it for guests as well. Its rich flavour, yet frugal ingredients, are truly delicious. Serve with bread, cheese, and a crisp white wine.

Ingredients

3 yellow potatoes, peeled, diced into 1-inch (2.5 cm) cubes
3 garlic cloves, chopped
2 carrots, peeled, chopped
2 celery sticks, chopped
1 yellow onion, sliced
½ red bell pepper, sliced
1 can (28 oz/796 mL) plum tomatoes, roughly chopped
¼ cup water
¼ cup olive oil
1 tsp dried oregano
1¼ tsp salt
¼ tsp dried red chilies
Fresh cracked pepper
1 lb (500 g) cod
½ cup fresh parsley, chopped
¼ cup Kalamata olives, pitted, chopped

1. Add all of the ingredients, excluding the cod, parsley and olives, to a large 9-x12-inch (23x30 cm) casserole dish, with a fitted lid. Stir the ingredients together and place in the middle of a preheated oven, covered, for 50 minutes, or until the potatoes are almost cooked through.

2. Meanwhile, rinse the cod and press with paper towels to remove any excess water. Cut the cod into large 3-inch (7.5 cm) pieces.

3. Nestle the cod in the casserole cooking liquid. Add the parsley and olives and continue cooking, uncovered for 12-15 minutes, or until the fish is flaky. Serve hot with rustic bread.

Fresh vs. Frozen

Never frozen doesn't necessarily mean fresh; It simply means, never frozen. Often, frozen fish fillets are freshest because they have been flash frozen within hours of being caught. When buying frozen fillets check for freezer burn. The frozen pieces should have good colouring and shine to them. Frozen fillets also offer great convenience since they are often packed in suitable portion sizes. If going the fresh route, ask when the fish was caught. Fish should never have a strong odour!

Substitutions

Cod can be substituted with any lean, firm white fish such as haddock, halibut or sea bass.

Bake 425°F / 220°C | Serves 4 | Time to Table 1½ hours | Diet v gf

3 greek sisters

CHESTNUT STIFADO

Stifado Me Kastana (Stee-FAH-doh Meh KA-stah-nah)

Stifado is one of our favourite Greek stews. It is a fragrant onion and meat stew popular throughout Greece. We wondered if the depth of flavour that is achieved when stewing meat with wine, could also be obtained in a meatless variation. Yes it can! Meaty chestnuts and mushrooms do the trick in this vegetarian Stifado. Delicious.

1. Add the chestnuts to a pot with cold water and bring to a boil. Simmer the chestnuts for 3 minutes and remove from the heat. Remove one chestnut at a time from the boiling water and use a sharp knife to peel away the skin and any fuzzy parts. Once the chestnuts have cooled, the skin becomes difficult to remove so keeping them in the hot water helps to facilitate with the removal of the skin. Set aside.

2. In a blender or food processor, add the canned plum tomatoes and process until smooth. Set aside.

3. Heat the olive oil in large pot over medium heat. Add the minced shallots and sauté until soft, about 3 minutes. Add the garlic and sauté for a minute further. Add the whole shallots, mushrooms and Mavrodaphne and stir. Bring to a boil over high heat.

4. Add the salt, paprika, cinnamon, cloves, all spice berries and bay leaves and stir. Add the 1 cup puréed tomato sauce with the water and bring to a boil. Reduce the heat to medium low and simmer, partially covered for 35 minutes.

5. Taste and adjust the seasonings before serving. Top with fresh cracked pepper, remove the bay leaves and serve with bread.

Ingredients
1 lb (500 g) chestnuts (about 40)
1 cup (8 oz/250 mL) canned plum tomatoes
¼ cup olive oil
2 shallots, minced
3 garlic cloves, roughly chopped
½ lb (250 g) shallots, peeled
½ lb (250 g) white button mushrooms
½ lb (250 g) cremini mushrooms
1 cup Mavrodaphne, or other dessert wine
1 tsp salt
1 tsp sweet paprika
1 cinnamon stick
6 whole cloves
3 all spice berries
2 bay leaves
1½ cups water
Fresh cracked pepper

Serves 4   Time to Table 1 ½ hours   Diet v gf

food is love

3 greek sisters

LENTIL BURGERS

Keftedakia Me Fakies (Keh-fteh-DAH-kee-ah Meh Fah-kee-ES)

This burger is flavourful, healthy, and it won't leave you feeling like you cheated yourself out of eating something heartier. Dress it up with roasted peppers, cheese, and anything else you fancy. Your body will thank you.

1 Heat the olive oil in a medium saucepan over medium heat. Add the onion and sauté until soft, about 5 minutes. Add the garlic and cook for one minute further. Add the rice and vegetable stock and bring to a boil. Reduce the heat and simmer, covered, until rice is cooked through, about 20 minutes. Transfer to a large bowl and set aside to cool.

2 Once cooled, add the remaining ingredients and use a masher to mix the ingredients together thoroughly and break up the lentils. Shape into 8 thick patties, about ½-inch (1 cm) thick and brush both sides with olive oil.

3 Heat a cast-iron skillet over medium heat. Place the patties in the hot skillet and cook until the patties are browned and crisp, about 4-5 minutes per side. Use a spatula to flip patties and help re-shape them while cooking. Serve lentil burgers on a favourite bun and enjoy with toppings of your choice.

Ingredients
2 tbsp olive oil
1 yellow onion, chopped
3 garlic cloves, minced
½ cup Arborio rice
1¾ cup vegetable stock
½ tsp dried oregano
½ tsp salt
Fresh cracked pepper
½ cup walnut crumbs, toasted
1 can (19 oz/540 mL) lentils, drained and rinsed
¼ cup breadcrumbs
2 tbsp fresh squeezed lemon juice
1 tbsp balsamic vinegar
2 tbsp fresh parsley, chopped
2 tbsp fresh mint, chopped
Olive oil for greasing

Make Ahead
The patty mixture can be prepared and stored in the refrigerator on the morning of serving day.

Gluten Friendly
Use gluten-free breadcrumbs to make this recipe completely gluten-free.

Makes 8 Time to Table 1 hour Diet v

food is love

3 greek sisters

LEEK PIE FILLING

Prassopita (Prah-SOH-pee-tah)

There is an abundance of leeks, herbs and spinach in this recipe, so you will be putting in some time on the cutting board, but your labour will be rewarded. Prassopita, or leek pie, is delicious. This pie can be made with both prepared phyllo or homemade phyllo. Both options make for a delicious lunch or light supper.

1 Consider your phyllo pie of choice. Prepare homemade phyllo, or thaw prepared phyllo and set aside.

2 For the filling, heat the olive oil in a large pot over medium heat. Add the leeks, scallions, salt and sauté until soft, about 5 minutes. Add the garlic and sauté a minute further. Add the spinach a handful at a time, until it has wilted and reduced in volume. Remove from the heat once the juices released have evaporated. Transfer ingredients to a colander and press with a wooden spoon to help drain any excess juices.

3 Transfer ingredients to a large bowl, add the feta cheese, dill, parsley, eggs and mix.

Your filling is now complete and ready to be added to a phyllo pastry of your choice.

To place this filling in a homemade phyllo pie refer to page 229 for preparation and cooking instructions.

To place this filling in a homemade spiral pie refer to page 233 for preparation and cooking instructions.

To place this filling in a prepared phyllo pastry refer to page 237 for preparation and cooking instructions.

Make Ahead
This filling can be prepared and stored in the refrigerator up to 1 day in advance.

Ingredients
1 phyllo pie of choice, page 229, 233 or 237
¼ cup olive oil
5 large leeks, both white & pale green parts, thinly sliced
5 scallions, both white & green, chopped
¼ tsp salt
4 garlic cloves, minced
2 bunches spinach, roughly chopped
2 cups feta cheese, crumbled
½ cup fresh dill, chopped
⅓ cup fresh parsley, chopped
2 eggs

Serves 6-8　Time to Table for filling 45 min　Diet v

food is love

After Dinner

Lemon Yogurt Loaf
Lemon Ice Cream
Karidopita
Chocolate Walnut Cake
Diples
Sour-Cherry Spoon Sweet
Quince Spoon Sweet
Grape Spoon Sweet
Halva
Yogurt Mousse
Pantespani
Revani
Pasteli
Rice Pudding
Vanilia
Chestnuts
Mountain Tea
Mulled Wine

LEMON YOGURT LOAF

Tourta Meh Lemoni Ke Yiaourti (TOUR-tah Meh Leh-MOH-nee Keh Yia-OOR-tee)

This loaf is light and fluffy and its lemony glaze has the perfect zing. It is made with Greek yogurt, which is packed with protein, and olive oil instead of butter. This recipe makes great cupcakes as well.

Ingredients
1½ cups all-purpose flour
¾ cup sugar
2 tsp baking powder
¼ tsp salt
Zest of 1 lemon, grated
1 cup Greek yogurt
2 eggs
⅓ cup olive oil
1 tsp vanilla extract
Olive oil for greasing

For the Glaze
½ cup Confectioner's sugar
3 tbsp fresh squeezed lemon juice

1. Stir the flour, sugar, baking powder, salt and lemon zest in a small bowl. Set aside.

2. In a separate large bowl, whisk the yogurt and the eggs together. Continue whisking and slowly add the olive oil, followed by the vanilla. Whisk until the ingredients are fully combined.

3. Add the flour mixture set aside earlier to the yogurt mixture ½ cup at a time. Use a rubber spatula to mix the ingredients together until combined.

4. Transfer the thick batter to a lightly greased 9-x5-inch (2L) loaf pan. Place in the middle of a preheated oven for 40 minutes or until cake is light golden-brown in colour and a knife inserted into the centre of the cake comes out clean.

5. Leaving the loaf in the pan, set it aside to cool on a rack for 10 minutes.
Run a knife along the edge of the loaf to loosen it from the pan. Turn the pan over and remove the loaf.

6. To prepare the glaze, whisk the sugar and lemon juice in a small bowl until combined. Brush the glaze over the surface of the loaf using a pastry brush. Serve.

Variation
Make Lemon Yogurt Cupcakes by placing the batter in a lined muffin tray. Bake for 30 minutes.

Make Ahead
This loaf can be prepared up to 1 day in advance.

3 greek sisters

Bake (350°F / 180°C) Serves (6-8) Time to Table (1 hour) Diet (v)

food is love

LEMON ICE CREAM

Pagoto Lemoni (Pah-go-TOH Leh-MOH-nee)

Greeks love lemons, so this had to be done. Lemon is a vibrant and refreshing ice cream flavour. It can be enjoyed plain or garnished with dark chocolate shavings and lemon zest.

Ingredients
3 egg yolks
¾ cup sugar
1 cup whole milk, warmed to 180°F (82°C)
2 cups whipping cream
½ cup fresh squeezed lemon juice
½ tsp vanilla extract

1. **Day 1**
In the bowl of a stand-mixer fitted with a whisk attachment, whisk the egg yolks and sugar on medium speed until smooth and lighter in colour, about 2 minutes. Lower the speed and slowly add the warmed milk. Once thoroughly mixed, transfer to a saucepan and place on stovetop over medium heat. Whisking frequently, remove mixture from heat as soon as it reaches a low-boil. Transfer to a large bowl.

2. Add the whipping cream, lemon juice and vanilla extract to the large bowl and whisk ingredients together. Cover the bowl and place in a refrigerator. Chill for 8 hours or up to overnight.

3. **Day 2**
Remove the mixture from the refrigerator and stir with a wooden spoon.

4. Slowly pour the mixture into a working ice cream maker. Stir until thickened, about 10-15 minutes. (Be sure to follow your Ice Cream Maker's instructions during this step.)

5. Serve at once or if you prefer a firmer ice cream transfer to an airtight container and store in the freezer for 4-6 hours or overnight.

Make Ahead
Lemon ice cream can be stored in an airtight container in the freezer for up to 1 month in advance; however, the intensity of the lemon flavor will decrease the longer it sits in the freezer.

3 greek sisters

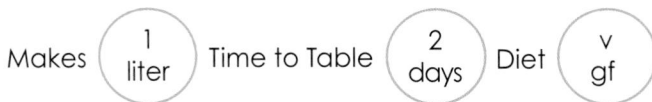

Makes (1 liter) Time to Table (2 days) Diet (v gf)

food is love

Variations
Add either toasted or untoasted walnuts as a cake topper.

Add a dollop of Yogurt Mousse, page 183, for a new and
refreshing take on an old and timeless dessert.

3 greek sisters

KARIDOPITA

(Kah-ree-DOH-pee-tah)

The use of walnuts, cinnamon, and cloves seem endless in the Greek kitchen. Here they come together again for yet another classic dessert. This version of Karidopita, given to us by one of our dear aunts, is sweetened with a cinnamon-scented syrup and a splash of lemon - surprised?

1. Place the syrup ingredients in a small saucepan and bring to a boil over high heat. Stir using a wooden spoon until the sugar has dissolved. Reduce the heat to medium and maintain a low-boil for 5 minutes. Remove from the heat and set aside to cool completely.

2. In the mixing bowl of a stand-mixer fitted with a whisk attachment add the egg-yolks, sugar and brandy. Whisk on medium-high speed until mixture is smooth and light yellow in colour, about 2 minutes. On low speed add the orange juice, mix for 30 seconds. Transfer to a large bowl, add the orange zest and set this wet mixture aside.

3. In a food processor, add the walnuts and the remaining dry ingredients. Process until the walnuts are crumbs. Using a rubber spatula, fold the dry ingredients into the wet mixture set aside earlier. Set batter aside.

4. In the mixing bowl of a stand-mixer fitted with a whisk attachment add the egg whites and whisk on medium-high speed until stiff white peaks form. Using a rubber spatula, fold the whipped egg whites into the batter a third at a time until thoroughly incorporated and no white streaks remain.

5. Pour batter into a buttered, squared 9-inch (23 cm) baking pan and place in the middle of a preheated oven for 30 minutes, or until the cake is brown and pulls away from the sides of the pan and a knife comes out clean when inserted into the centre of the cake.

6. Leaving the warm cake in its pan, use a toothpick to prick the surface of cake in several spots. Pour the cooled syrup over the surface of the cake a little bit at a time, waiting for the syrup to be absorbed in between each round. Set cake aside to cool. Cut on a diagonal to create diamond-shaped pieces and serve.

Ingredients

For the syrup
1 cup water
1 cup sugar
2 tbsp fresh squeezed lemon juice
1 strip of lemon rind
1 cinnamon stick
2 whole cloves

For the cake batter
5 eggs, separated
½ cup sugar
2 tbsp Metaxa, or other brandy
¼ cup fresh squeezed orange juice
1 tbsp orange zest
1½ cups walnuts
½ cup breadcrumbs
3 tsp baking powder
2 tbsp all-purpose flour, sifted
½ tsp ground cinnamon
¼ tsp ground cloves
¼ tsp salt
Butter for greasing bakeware

Bake 350°F / 180°C | Serves 8 | Time to Table 1 hour | Diet v

food is love

CHOCOLATE WALNUT CAKE

Karidopita Me Sokolata (Kah-ree-DOH-pee-tah Meh Soh-koh-LAH-tah)

We feel that Greeks do not eat enough chocolate. Here, we have taken the classic Greek walnut cake, Karidopita, to a whole new level with a hint of cocoa and chocolate sauce. Change is hard on some, for traditional Karidopita calmly turn to page 167.

Ingredients

For the Syrup
⅔ cup water
⅔ cup sugar
1 tbsp unsweetened cocoa powder

For the Cake Batter
5 eggs, separated
½ cup sugar
2 tbsp Metaxa, or other brandy
¼ cup fresh squeezed orange juice
1 tbsp orange zest
1½ cups walnuts
½ cup breadcrumbs
2 tbsp all purpose flour, sifted
2 tbsp unsweetened cocoa powder
3 tsp baking powder
½ tsp ground cinnamon
¼ tsp ground cloves
¼ tsp salt
Butter for greasing bakeware

For the Topping
2 tbsp walnut crumbs, toasted

1. Place the syrup ingredients in a small saucepan and bring to a boil over high heat. Stir using a wooden spoon until the sugar has dissolved. Reduce the heat to medium and maintain a low-boil for 5 minutes. Remove from the heat and set aside to cool completely.

2. In the mixing bowl of a stand-mixer fitted with a whisk attachment add the egg-yolks, sugar and brandy. Whisk on medium-high speed until mixture is smooth and light yellow in colour, about 2 minutes. On low speed add the orange juice, and mix for 30 seconds. Transfer to a large bowl, add the orange zest and set this wet mixture aside.

3. In a food processor, add the walnuts and the remaining dry ingredients. Process until the walnuts are crumbs. Using a rubber spatula, fold the dry ingredients into the wet mixture set aside earlier. Set this batter aside.

4. In the mixing bowl of a stand-mixer fitted with a whisk attachment add the egg whites and whisk on medium-high speed until stiff white peaks form. Using a rubber spatula, fold the whipped egg whites into the batter a third at a time until thoroughly incorporated and no white streaks remain.

5. Pour batter into a buttered 8-inch (2 L) springform pan and place in the middle of a preheated oven for 35 minutes, or until the cake pulls away from the sides of the pan and a knife comes out clean when inserted into the centre of the cake.

6. Leaving the warm cake in its pan, use a toothpick to prick the surface of cake in several spots. Pour the cooled syrup over the surface of the cake a little bit at a time, waiting for the syrup to be absorbed in between each round. Set cake aside to cool on a cooling rack. *Continued on next page.*

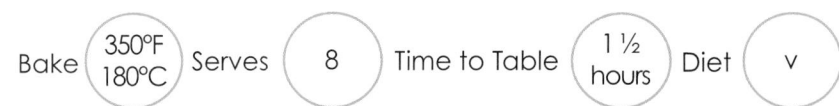

Bake 350°F 180°C | Serves 8 | Time to Table 1½ hours | Diet v

food is love

After Dinner 193

CHESTNUTS

Kastana (KAH-stah-nah)

Chestnuts, or kastana in Greek, are a favourite winter nut in our homes. Roasted chestnuts, a glass of red wine, and family and friends make for a perfect gathering.

There is a town in Thessaly, Greece that has chestnut trees growing in abundance, hence the name of the town, *Kastania*. Chestnuts can be found roasting on the streets and also in many local dishes.

Chestnuts can be roasted or boiled, it all depends on what you intend to do with them. When cooked, chestnuts have a sweet flavour. They contain no cholesterol, very little fat and no gluten.

3 greek sisters

Removing the Shell of Chestnuts by Boiling

Add the chestnuts to a pot with cold water and bring to a boil. Then simmer the chestnuts for 3 minutes. Remove pot from heat. Remove chestnuts one at a time, and with a sharp knife peel off the skin. Once chestnuts have cooled, the skin becomes difficult to remove so keep them in the hot water to facilitate the removal of the skin. Remove the fuzzy skin that sometimes sticks to the fruit as well. These chestnuts can then be added to recipes where they will continue to cook, e.g. a stew, a turkey stuffing, etc.

Boiling Chestnuts

If you want the chestnuts completely cooked, simmer for 20 minutes, then peel and use. Chestnuts may fall apart when removing the skin. These chestnuts can be mashed and added to recipes.

Roasting Chestnuts

Chestnuts need to be scored with a sharp knife before roasting. Make an "X" or a horizontal slash on the tip of each nut, as this will prevent the chestnuts from exploding in your oven. It will also make them easier to peel. Place on a baking sheet in a preheated 400°F (200°C) oven for 15-20 minutes. Serve warm.

Tip

When buying chestnuts, look for healthy looking nuts that feel heavy, with no apparent holes in them. Buy a few more nuts than a recipe calls for, as some nuts may be spoiled.

food is love

MOUNTAIN TEA

Tsai Tou Vounou (Ts-AH-ee Too Voo-NOO)

One of the best ways to warm up on cold nights is to enjoy Greek Mountain Tea, or "Tsai Tou Vounou". It is sometimes called "Shepherd's Tea". This tea needs very little to grow: little water, little soil.

According to our yiayia, this tea is miraculous. It cures the common cold, it helps with sore throats, it makes an achy body feel better, and it even boosts your immune system.   Who could argue - most people in the villages live to almost a hundred years old. They must be doing something right.

As the name suggests, mountain tea grows in the mountains. In our dad's village, high on the mountaintops, about 1000 meters above sea level, you can find this tea growing in the wild. The Sideritis plant, literally meaning "with iron", (hence the common name, ironwort), is picked and dried. The leaves, stalks and flowers are all added to a pot of hot water and brought to a boil. The mixture is left to boil for 5 minutes and then the tea is strained. Most Greeks add honey, but sugar can also be added if desired, or even a slice of lemon. The tea tastes herby, lemony and is caffeine-free.

This tea is inexpensive and sold in every Greek specialty shop. A warm cup of tea takes us back to those wonderful days and nights in Kalamata.

food is love

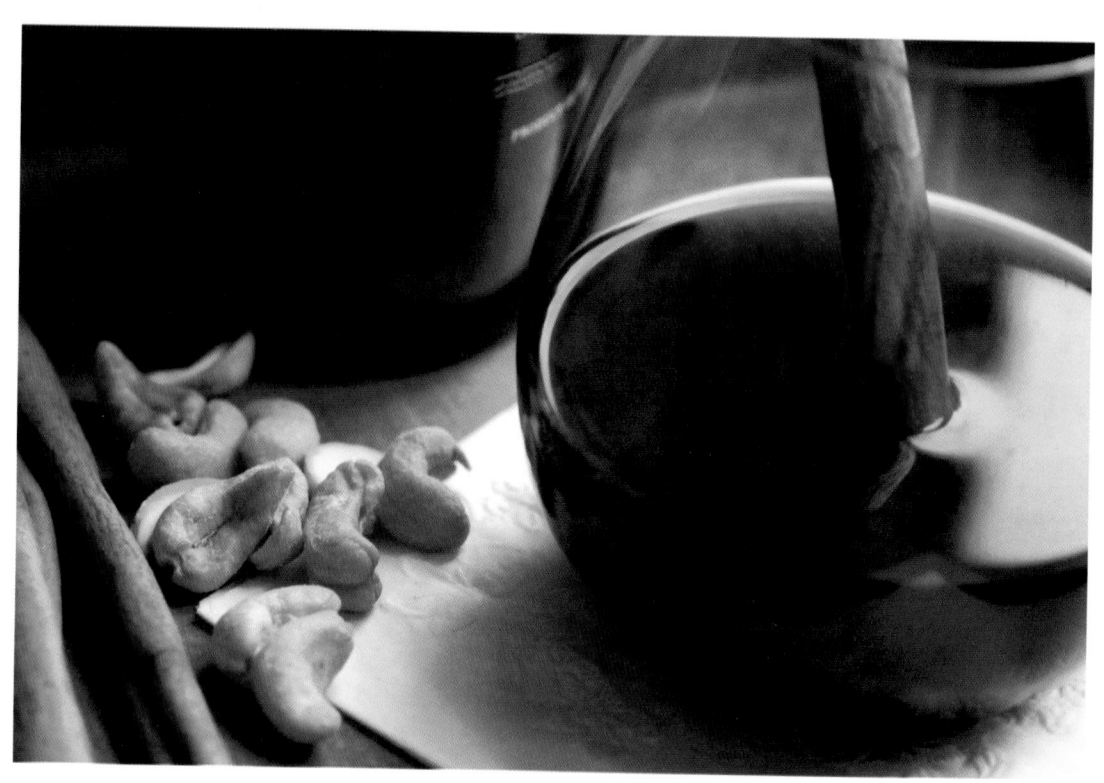

3 greek sisters

MULLED WINE

For centuries mulled wines have been warming hearts throughout Europe. This tradition of sweetening, warming and spicing red wine continues to this day and is a wonderful way to fill your home with intoxicating aromas. It is the perfect way to warm up friends and family during the cold winter nights and a great alternative to cider, eggnog or coffee.

Add all the ingredients to a large pot and heat through for 10-15 minutes until the honey has been dissolved. Do not bring to a boil. Once heated, ladle into mugs and serve warm.

Ingredients
1 bottle red Greek wine
⅓ cup Greek honey
¼ cup brandy, Metaxa preferred
Cinnamon stick
Orange rind
3 allspice berries
5 cloves

Substitution
Honey can be substituted with sugar if desired.

Sweetness
Once you have tried this recipe, you can always adjust sweetness to suit your liking.

Wine
An inexpensive bottle of wine will do just fine in a mulled wine recipe.

Serves 4-6   Time to Table 20 min   Diet v gf

food is love

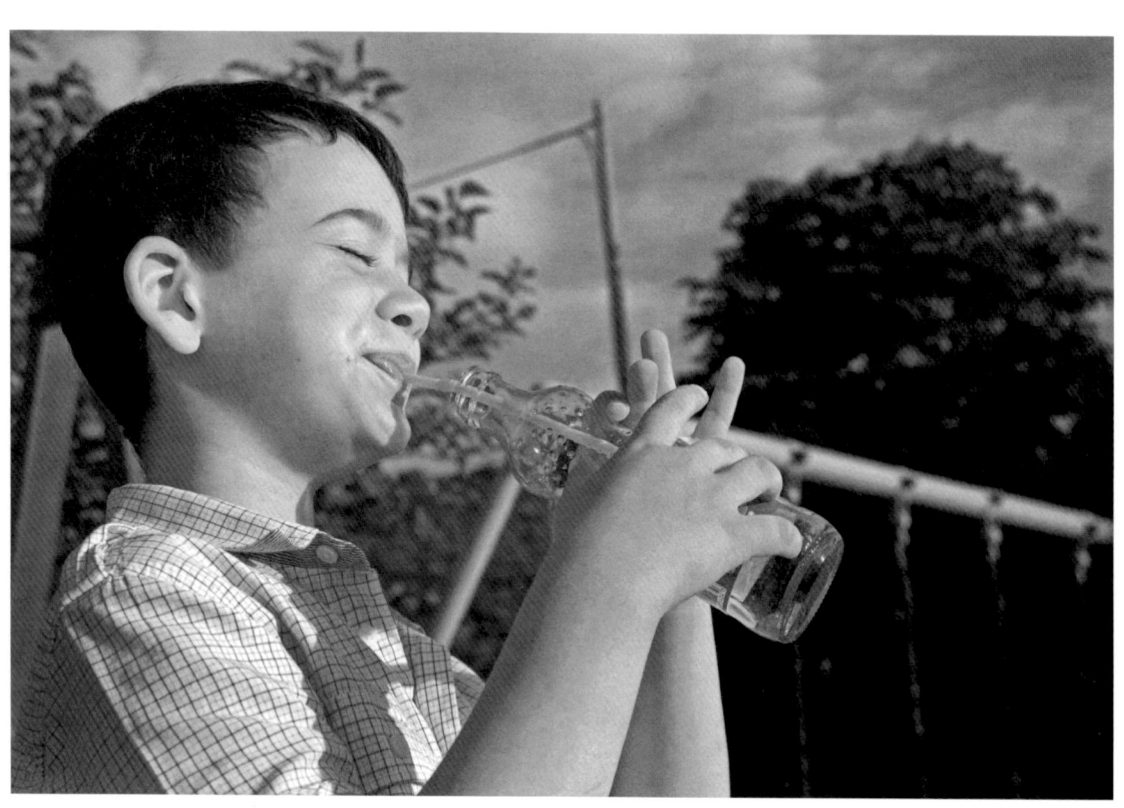

FLATBREAD

Lagana (Lah-GAH-nah)

Lagana bread is traditionally eaten on Clean Monday, Kathari Deftera, the first day of Lent that follows a weekend of festivities in March (Apokries). During Apokries people dress in costumes and party all day and night in anticipation of the 40 days of Lent that are to follow. We enjoy this bread so much, and it is so easy to prepare, that we make it more often than just on Clean Monday. Lagana closely resembles Italian Focaccia bread. They are both all-purpose flatbreads that taste great on their own, or alongside your favourite meal. The sprinkling of coarse salt and sesame seeds makes every bite delicious!

Ingredients
1½ cups warm water
2½ tsp active dry yeast
½ tsp salt
½ cup olive oil, plus extra for coating & greasing
3½ cups all-purpose flour, plus ½ cup reserve
1 tbsp sesame seeds
Coarse sea salt

1. In the bowl of a stand-mixer fitted with a dough-hook attachment add the warm water, yeast and salt. Mix with a wooden spoon until combined. Set aside until foamy, about 5-10 minutes. If mixture does not foam, discard and start over.

2. With the stand-mixer running add the olive oil and flour and knead on low speed until a dough forms.

3. Transfer dough to a lightly floured work surface and knead until there are no more sticky spots. Turn the dough into a ball and coat with about 2 tablespoons olive oil. Set aside in a warm draft-free spot for 1½ to 2 hours, or until the dough has doubled in size.

4. Transfer risen dough to a greased baking sheet and punch down. Using your fingers, gently flatten the dough until it is about ¾-inch (2 cm) thick.

5. Firmly press the back of a fork over the entire surface of the dough to create deep grooves. This will prevent the crust from rising too quickly and separating from the rest of the loaf. Sprinkle generously with sesame seeds and some coarse sea salt and place in the middle of a preheated oven for 15 minutes, or until bread is golden brown. Serve warm or at room temperature.

Bake 425°F 220°C | Makes 1 | Time to Table 2½ hours | Diet v

food is love

Make Ahead
Walnut and Olive Spelt bread can be stored in a freezer bag and will keep in a freezer for up to 3 months. Remove loaf from the freezer bag and set aside on kitchen towel to thaw before serving.

3 greek sisters

SPELT BREAD WITH WALNUTS & OLIVES

Psomi Me Karidia Ke Elies (Psoh-MEE Meh Kah-REE-dee-ah Keh Ee-lee-EHS)

We love to bake our own bread. It is the most basic of foods and many Greeks believe that the dinner table should have a loaf of bread ready to be broken with family and friends.
This bread recipe uses spelt, an ancient grain, with a slightly nutty flavour. Spelt flour lends a rustic quality to this walnut and olive bread recipe.

Ingredients
2½ tsp active dry yeast
2 cups warm water
1 tsp salt
5 cups whole spelt flour, plus
¾ cup reserve
2 tbsp olive oil
½ cup walnuts, roughly chopped
½ cup Kalamata olives, pitted and sliced
Olive oil for greasing

1. In the mixing bowl of a stand mixer fitted with a dough-hook attachment add the yeast and 1 cup of the warm water. Mix with a wooden spoon until the yeast has dissolved. Let mixture rest for 5-10 minutes until foamy. If your mixture does not foam, discard and start over.

2. With the stand-mixer running, add the remaining water to the mixing bowl. Add the salt and 1 cup of the flour and knead on low speed. Add the remaining four cups of flour, one cup at a time.

3. Add 1 tablespoon of the olive oil and continue kneading until incorporated. At this point, you should have a workable dough.

4. Transfer dough to a flat work surface and knead for 2 minutes with your hands. Add enough of the reserve flour so that your dough is no longer sticky. Flatten dough slightly and sprinkle evenly with the walnuts and olives. Fold over and gently knead dough until olives and walnuts are evenly distributed throughout the dough.

5. Turn dough into a ball, coat with remaining one tablespoon olive oil. Transfer to a bowl and cover with a cloth. Set aside in a warm, draft-free spot for 1½ hours until dough almost doubles in size.

6. Transfer dough to a flat work surface. Punch down and knead dough for 2-3 minutes. Divide dough in half and turn into two balls. Place on a greased baking sheet. Cover loosely with cloth and set-aside again in a warm, draft-free spot for 1 hour.

7. Dust tops of loaves with spelt flour and place in the middle of a preheated oven for 30-35 minutes until the bread is brown and sounds hollow when tapped. Transfer to a cooling rack. Serve warm or at room temperature.

Bake (425°F / 220°C) Makes (2) Time to Table (3½ hours) Diet (v)

food is love

CHRISTMAS BREAD

Christopsomo (Hree-STOH-psoh-moh)

This traditional Christmas loaf is made with only the finest ingredients and showcases brandy-soaked raisins. Traditions such as baking special recipes over the holidays are always a good idea that your family and friends will remember.

Ingredients
1 cup Sultana raisins
5 tbsp Metaxa, or other brandy
5 tbsp hot water
2 cups milk, warmed to 115°F (45°C)
7½ cups all-purpose flour, plus ½ cup reserve
2½ tsp active dry yeast
1 cup sugar
½ cup walnut halves, roughly chopped
2 tsp anise seed
1 tsp ground cinnamon
1 tsp orange zest
1 tsp mastic powder
½ tsp salt
4 eggs, room temperature, lightly beaten
1 stick (8 tbsp, 4oz) unsalted butter, melted
Olive oil for greasing baking sheet
1 egg yolk
2 tbsp milk
Sesame seeds for sprinkling (optional)

1. **Day 1**
In a large glass bowl, add the raisins, brandy and 5 tablespoons hot water. Cover and set aside on counter overnight.

2. **Day 2**
In a medium-sized bowl add 1 cup of the milk, 1 cup of the flour and the yeast. Stir and set aside for 1-2 hours until the mixture is light, fluffy and full of holes, like a sponge.

3. Sift the remaining flour in the bowl of a stand-mixer fitted with a dough-hook attachment. Continue by adding the sugar, walnuts, anise seed, cinnamon, zest, mastic powder and salt. Stir with a wooden spoon. Drain the raisins from the brandy and add to the bowl.

4. Create a well in the centre and add the eggs, butter, remaining cup of warmed milk and the sponge that was set aside earlier. Knead on low speed until a dough forms. Transfer to a flat work surface and continue kneading with your hands, using the reserve flour if necessary. Set dough aside in a warm draft-free spot until the dough has doubled in size, at least 1 hour.

5. Transfer the dough to a flat work surface, punch down and knead for about 1 minute. Cut away about 2 cups of dough and turn it into a ball. This piece will later be used to decorate the loaf. Cover with a cloth and set aside. Turn the largest piece of dough into a ball and arrange in the middle of an 8-inch (2 L) round greased baking pan. Cover with a cloth and set aside in a warm draft-free spot until the dough has doubled in size and has filled the entire baking pan. *Continued on next page.*

3 greek sisters

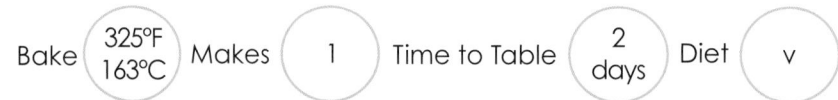

Bake 325°F 163°C Makes 1 Time to Table 2 days Diet v

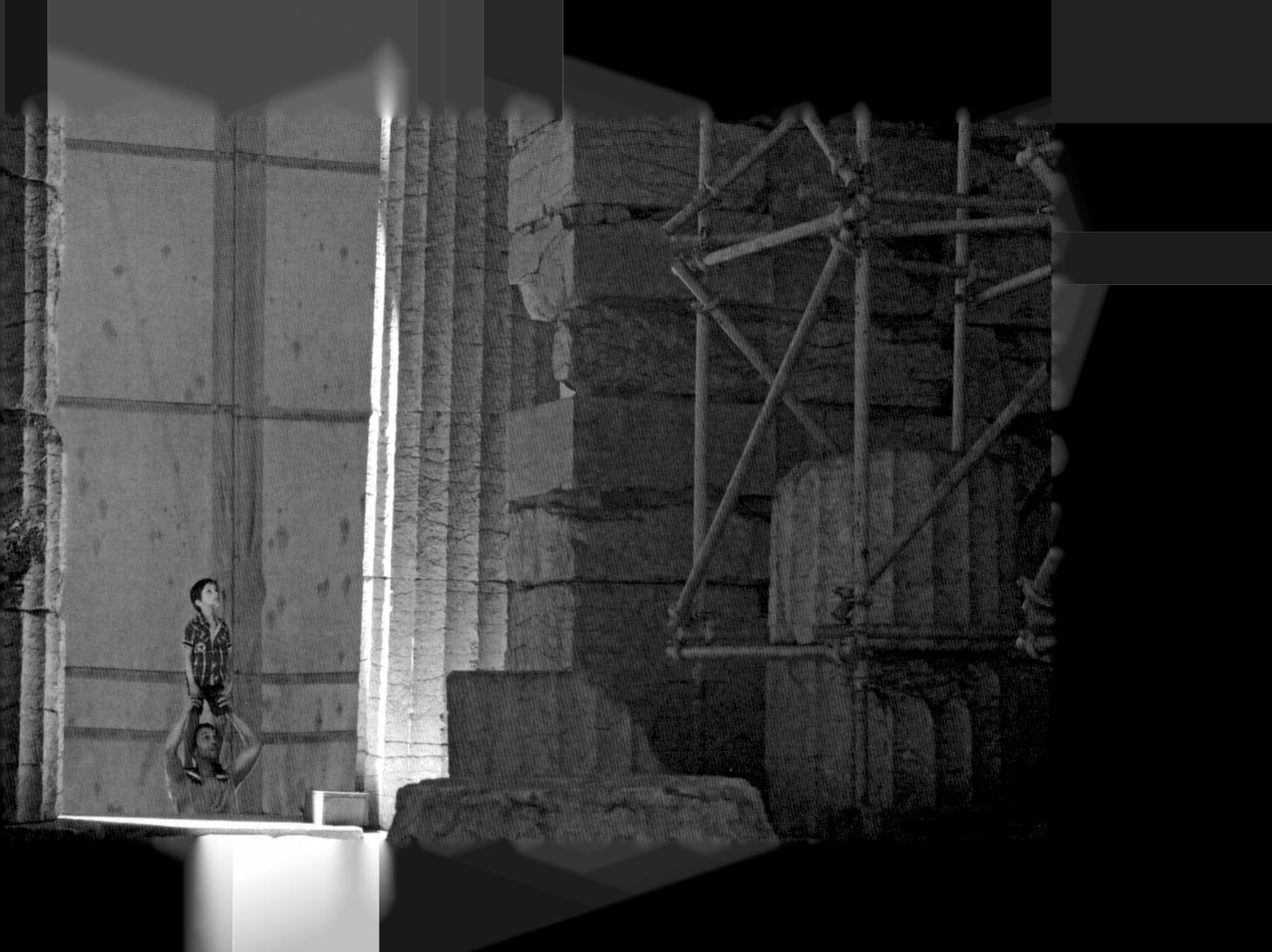

Labouring hands are bold and strong, they can overcome what the weak

eye can't even comprehend.

- Greek adage

Το μάτι δειλό, μα το χέρι τολμηρό.

EGG NOODLES

Hilopites (Hee-loh-PEE-tes)

Home-made hilopites are like snowflakes, no two are exactly alike. The size and shape of each square-shaped pasta depends on the cook's deftness with his/her knife.

Back in the day, hilopites were made in vast amounts. Kilos of flour and dozens of eggs were kneaded into dough. There was so much dough in fact, that it was too difficult to knead by hand. Our grandparents would lay clean sheets over the dough and step on it – much like grape stomping. Many hands were needed to get this dough rolled into thin sheets and then cut into square pieces. The pasta was laid out on clean sheets to dry in the sun for days. The longer it dried, the better. After that, they were kept in a cool dry place to be used in various dishes throughout the winter.

Below is a recipe for a small batch of hilopites. It is worth trying, if only just to gain an appreciation for the convenience and price of pasta at your local grocery store.

Ingredients
1 kg all-purpose flour (plus 1 cup reserve for dusting)
1 tsp salt
7 eggs, lightly beaten
1 cup milk

1. Add the flour and salt to a large glass bowl and make a well in the centre. Add the eggs and the milk in the centre and use your hand to knead the ingredients together. If all of the flour does not become incorporated, add additional tablespoons of milk at a time. The dough will be hard to work with at first.

2. Dust a flat work surface with flour. Begin kneading the dough on the floured surface by pressing the heel of your hand into the dough away from you and then folding it in half, turning it a ¼-turn and repeating the pressing and folding. This is repeated over and over until the dough is slightly elastic. Let the dough rest for 15 minutes.

3. Divide the dough into 15 small balls. Prepare your pasta machine on a sturdy table and set the dial to the widest setting, usually labelled number 1. Flatten the ball of dough with your hands and feed it through the roller. Fold the piece of dough together and feed it through the roller again. Repeat with the remaining pieces of dough.

4. Change the roller dial setting to number 2 and feed each piece through the roller. This time the pieces of dough will become even longer. As the dough pieces become longer, it becomes a task that is easier to do with a partner. If the pieces become too long, cut them in half so that this task is more manageable. Dust the dough pieces with flour if they begin sticking to the rollers. Always lay the pieces flat on the table. *Continued on next page.*

Makes (1 kg) Time to Table (2 days) Diet (v)

food is love

Egg Noodle recipe continued from previous page.

5   Change the dial to number 5 and feed each piece through the roller.

6   Attach the noodle cutting attachment to the pasta machine. Feed each piece through the roller and hang them on a clean drying rack. Ensure that the pasta strips are not touching as they will stick together.

7   Egg noodles can be left on the drying rack for long strips of noodles or they can be cut into small square-shaped noodles. To cut the noodles, lay the pasta strips on a cutting board and use a sharp knife to cut small square-shaped pasta. Arrange the cut pasta on a clean pan that has been lightly dusted with flour or cornmeal, so that they do not stick. Let the noodles dry for 2-3 days before cooking.

_____

Make Ahead
Noodles can be stored in an airtight container in the pantry for up to 1 year.

3 greek sisters

YOGURT FETA PRESERVE

Armi (AR-mee)

Feta cheese usually comes packed in salted water, called brine. When feta cheese is submerged in brine, it can last for a very long time. Our family took this method of preservation a step further. Our grandparents and parents would add salt and olive oil to homemade yogurt and then immerse the feta cheese in this creamy mixture called Armi. This mixture did more than just preserve the feta, it added flavour and creaminess to the cheese. We aren't exactly sure if other parts of Greece use this method, or if it is simply a secret that was kept by our parents' villages, but we do know that once you try it, you will be switching your brine for Armi.

1 Select a feta storage container with a fitted lid. Add the yogurt and salt to the container and mix thoroughly. Add the olive oil and mix. Immerse the feta cheese so that it is completely covered with the yogurt mixture. Store in the refrigerator.

Ingredients
2 cups Homemade yogurt (see recipe page 224) or unstrained plain yogurt
1 tbsp salt
2 tbsp olive oil
1 lb (500 g) feta cheese

Substitution
Unstrained yogurt refers to homemade yogurt or a Balkan-style yogurt. Strained yogurt or Greek yogurt is too thick to make Armi.

Make Ahead
Yogurt Feta Preserve will keep in the refrigerator for 2 months.

Time to Table (15 min) Diet (v gf)

food is love

When waiting for the yogurt to cool to 120°F (50°C) our mom did not use a thermometer. With enough experience she knew when the milk was ready for the starter culture. She would simply insert a clean finger in the milk. If she was able to keep her finger in the milk and count to ten, then she knew the milk was ready. If her finger could not withstand the count to 10, then she knew it needed to cool further. Our mom has a higher tolerance for heat than we do. Our fingers can never get past 3 seconds! So we recommend using a thermometer and letting the milk cool to 120°F (50°C).

3 greek sisters

HOMEMADE YOGURT

Yiaourti (Yee-ah-OOR-tee)

Yogurt is so popular in Greece that people enjoy eating it throughout the day. It is served for breakfast as a snack, and even dessert. Greek yogurt has a distinctive tang and twice the protein of other yogurts. There are no thickeners, gelatins, additives or preservatives. Blankets piled over large bowls in the corner of our parents' dining room was a tell-tale sign that yogurt was prepared that day. Our parents made yogurt regularly; it's significant to the Greek diet. The only tool you will need when making yogurt is a thermometer, unless you are like our parents, and can insert your finger into scalding liquid without consequence.

1 Add the homo milk and cream to a large pot over high heat stirring often to avoid burning. Remove the pot from the heat once a thermometer registers 180°F (82°C). The milk will be foamy at the top.

2 Set the pot aside until milk cools to 120°F (50°C).

3 Add the starter culture to the tepid milk and gently stir. Transfer the milk to sterilized containers. Cover with several clean kitchen towels and set aside in a warm draft-free spot for at least 6 hours or overnight.

4 Transfer the set yogurt containers to the refrigerator. Serve chilled.

Starter Culture
Be sure to save some of this yogurt as the starter culture for your next homemade batch.

Milk Temperature
It is imperative that the milk reaches 180°F (82°C) as this temperature kills the bacteria in the milk and alters the milk protein which allows it to thicken into yogurt. If your milk goes above 180°F (82°C) it will burn and lend a bad taste to your yogurt. Keep a close eye!

Ingredients
3 L organic, homo milk
1 L 10% cream
Starter culture (¼ cup yogurt diluted with 2 tbsp milk)

Greek Yogurt
Homemade yogurt can be strained by placing it in a cheesecloth or fine-mesh strainer over a bowl. Set it aside in the refrigerator to strain for at least 4 hours. This will remove the excess whey and will thicken the yogurt even more, making it Greek-style yogurt.

Optional
Instead of using kitchen towels to cover the milk containers, place the containers in your oven with the pilot light on. This will help to set the yogurt as well.

Makes (4 liters) Time to Table (1 day) Diet (v gf)

food is love

THE ART OF MAKING PHYLLO

Making phyllo is as simple as making your own pie crust, yet rumours of its difficulty abound. This recipe will quickly change that. This foolproof method will allow you to impress any Greek yiayia! Phyllo dough does not have yeast, so you do not have to wait for your dough to rise; however, you do need to wait for your dough to "rest". This resting phase is needed in order for your dough to stretch the length of your table. When dough does not successfully stretch, Greek women are often heard referring to their dough as "sick" or "unwell". The cure for this illness is simply giving your dough adequate time to rest. Set the dough aside, and come back to it later. With the passing of time, this dough will easily stretch and can be shaped into circular pies, rectangular pies, spirals, and triangles. All of these shapes can be stuffed with a variety of fillings. Regardless of shape and filling, this dough is always flaky and delicious. Once served, boasting is encouraged.

3 greek sisters

3 greek sisters

Rolling the Dough

Wrap the end of the dough around the pin, and place your hands on the centre of the pin. In a continuous motion, work your hands away from each other, while rolling the pin back and forth. With this motion, you are lengthening the dough till it almost covers the entire length of the dowel. This will take practise.

PHYLLO PIE TECHNIQUE

There are subtle variations in technique employed by Greek cooks to make their signature homemade phyllo. Some cooks credit their skilled hands, in other words, their ability to use their skinny dowel with such ease that they can spread the dough paper-thin. Other cooks give credit to their technique of layering their dough several times over and separating each layer with oil or butter. One thing is always true - a homemade pie is hailed a success when the colour of the pastry is a beautiful golden-brown and the crunch of each bite can be heard throughout the room. We have done our research, and have found that although there are many, many ways to make a flaky pie dough, the method described below is the most efficient, and it's fail-proof. Success is imminent!

1   Add 5 cups flour to a large bowl. Make a well in the centre and add the water, olive oil, vinegar and salt. Use your hands to mix the ingredients together until thoroughly incorporated and a dough forms.

2   Transfer the dough to a lightly-floured work surface and knead for two minutes. The dough should be soft and no longer sticky to the touch. Cover the dough and set it aside at room temperature for 1-1½ hours. This is a good time to choose and prepare your filling.

3   Divide your dough into 2 pieces, one slightly smaller. The smaller piece will be used for the bottom crust and the larger piece will be used for the top crust.

4   On a lightly floured large work surface, use a rolling pin to flatten the large piece of phyllo dough. Lift and turn the dough and continue rolling until you have a large circle about 24-inches (60 cm) in diameter.

5   Repeat this process and create a smaller round circle with the second, smaller piece of dough.

6   Using a pastry brush, add a liberal amount of fat (oil or butter, or a combination) to the entire surface of the dough. Let the dough rest for 30 minutes.

7   Pull at the end of one of the pieces of dough. It should stretch easily. Working from the centre of the dough, stretch and pull the dough until it is paper thin. Again, you will need a large work surface. If the dough does not stretch easily, let it rest for 10 minutes further. *Continued on next page.*

Ingredients
5 cups all-purpose flour
2 cups lukewarm water
¼ cup olive oil
3 tsp red wine vinegar
1½ tsp salt
1 cup reserve flour
1 cup fat (unsalted butter, melted or olive oil, see below)
1 Filling Recipe, cooled, page 119, 124 or 159.

Olive Oil vs. Butter
Perfect phyllo needs to be crunchy, therefore it needs fat. Fat adds moisture, flavour and crunchiness to phyllo. Butter, olive oil or vegetable oil are the most commonly used fats. For the richest flavour and crunchiest phyllo, use butter. Some cooks prefer olive oil or even corn oil to grease each layer. One reason is simply economical, the other, is simply the prefered taste. A mixture of butter and olive oil in equal proportions can also be used.

Bake 400°F / 200°C   Makes 1   Time to Table 4 hours

food is love

8 ·Liberally brush the paper-thin phyllo dough with more fat, then fold the dough together again. Fold the dough in thirds and brush any new surfaces of dough with more fat. Continue folding the dough and brushing with fat until the dough is a "ball" again. This technique creates many layers of phyllo that have all been brushed with fat to make the phyllo crunchy once it has been baked. Set aside for 30 minutes or until the fat has been reabsorbed in the dough and it is no longer runny.

9 Repeat with the second piece of dough. After this critical resting phase, the dough will be ready to be flattened once again.

10 Grease a round 16-inch (40 cm) baking pan and set aside.

11 Working with the smaller piece of dough first, use your rolling pin to flatten the dough until it is slightly larger than your baking pan. Transfer the dough to the pan allowing the excess dough to hang over the edges of the pan.

12 Add the filling of your choice to the pan.

13 Open the second, larger piece of dough until it is at least 2-inches (5 cm) larger than your baking pan. Place the dough on top of the filling. Pull at the dough to create a ruffled top.

14 Gather the excess dough hanging over the edge from the bottom crust and fold it up and over the top crust to seal the filling. Use your fingertips to firmly press the dough together.

15 Brush the top with fat and place in the middle of a preheated oven for 15 minutes. If the top crust has risen into a dome-shape, simply poke the top crust with a sharp knife to allow the steam to escape.

16 Reduce the heat to 350°F (180°C) and continue cooking for 30-40 minutes further, or until the crust is golden-brown.

Make Ahead

Any unused dough can be wrapped in wax paper and then placed in freezer bags and frozen. Will keep in the freezer for 6 months. Simply thaw on counter before using.

Uncooked phyllo pies can be frozen for up to 6 months. Simply thaw on counter for a few hours before cooking.

food is love

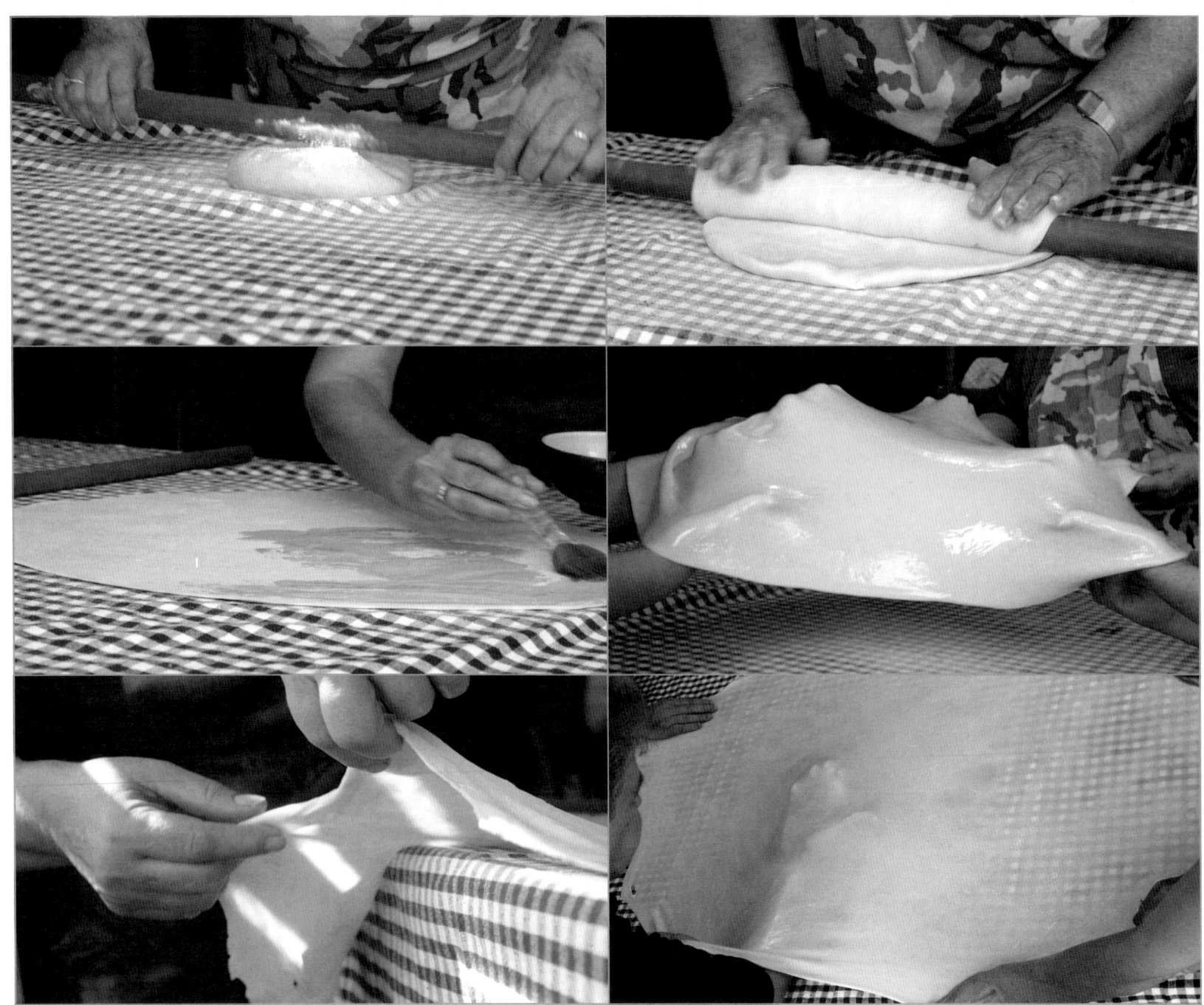

3 greek sisters

SPIRAL PHYLLO PIE TECHNIQUE

This spiral pie, resembling a snail's shell, is our favourite way to stretch and stuff phyllo. A standard rolling pin does the trick when opening this dough. We recommend opening the dough on a patterned tablecloth. As you begin to stretch the dough, it becomes thin enough to see the pattern of the tablecloth through it. At this point, the dough is ready to be stuffed and then coiled. These coils can be baked as individual spiral pies, or joined together to make larger impressive pies. There are a myriad of fillings to choose from - cheese, vegetables, or meat.

1 Add 5 cups flour to a large bowl. Make a well in the centre and add the water, olive oil, vinegar and salt. Use your hands to mix the ingredients together until thoroughly incorporated and a dough forms.

2 Transfer the dough to a lightly-floured work surface and knead for two minutes. The dough should be soft and no longer sticky to the touch. Cover the dough and set it aside at room temperature for 1-1½ hours. This is a good time to choose and prepare your filling.

3 Divide your phyllo dough into 8 equal pieces.

4 Cover a large table with a clean sheet or tablecloth. Dust the cloth with flour so that the dough does not stick to the cloth.

5 Take one of the balls of dough and use a rolling pin to flatten it. Lift and turn the dough and continue rolling until you have a large circle about 12-inches (30 cm) in diameter.

6 Repeat this process with the remaining 7 balls of dough.

7 Using a pastry brush, add a liberal amount of fat (oil or butter, or a combination) to the entire surface of each piece of dough. Let the dough rest for 30 minutes.

8 Pull at the end of a piece of dough. It should stretch easily. Working from the centre of that piece of dough, stretch and pull until it is paper thin. Again, you will need a large work surface. If the dough does not stretch easily, let it rest for 10 minutes further. *Continued on next page.*

Ingredients
5 cups all-purpose flour
2 cups lukewarm water
¼ cup olive oil
3 tsp red wine vinegar
1½ tsp salt
1 cup reserve flour
1 cup fat (unsalted butter, melted or olive oil, see below)
1 Filling Recipe, cooled, page 119, 124 or 159.

Olive Oil vs. Butter
Perfect phyllo needs to be crunchy, therefore it needs fat. Fat adds moisture, flavour and crunchiness to phyllo. Butter, olive oil or vegetable oil are the most commonly used fats. For the richest flavour and crunchiest phyllo, use butter. Some cooks prefer olive oil or even corn oil to grease each layer. One reason is simply economical, the other, is simply the prefered taste. A mixture of butter and olive oil in equal proportions can also be used.

food is love

Bake (400°F / 200°C) Makes (2) Time to Table (4 hours)

Spiral Phyllo Pie Technique recipe continued from previous page.

9   Grease two round 16-inch (40 cm) baking pans and set aside.

10 Add 1/8 of your filling of choice in three rows along the edge of the dough that is closest to you. Space the filling so that it resembles a checkerboard. Fold over the edge of the dough that is closest to you to cover the filling. Use a knife or pastry cutter to trim away the edges of the dough that are thick and untidy.

11 Grab the edge of the tablecloth that is closest to you and slowly lift it up. The phyllo should naturally roll forward onto itself. Continue lifting the tablecloth until the dough has completely rolled onto itself. Brush the roll with fat. Transfer the roll to the first baking pan and wrap the roll around itself to create a coil.

12 Repeat this process 7 more times until all of the phyllo and filling have been used.   Use 4 coils per baking pan.

13 Place in the middle of a preheated oven for 15 minutes. Reduce the heat to 350°F (180°C) and continue cooking for 30-40 minutes further, or until the crust is golden-brown.

Variations

When making a large spiral pie, each coil can have a different filling. This makes for an impressive pie. The first coil could be filled with cheese, the second with leeks, the third with chicken and the fourth with pork, or any other combination you desire.

You do not always have to make a large pie with all 4 coils. You can make 4 individual coils, cook what you need and freeze the rest for a later date. When ready to use, thaw coil and cook as you normally would.

3 greek sisters

Rolling Pins
The ideal rolling pin for phyllo dough must be both long and skinny. The ideal length is 30-inches (75 cm) and a diameter of about 3/4-inch (2 cm). The ends should be tapered. This tool will aid in the spreading of the phyllo so that it is paper-thin. Many cooks who cannot get their hands on one, simply use the ends of wooden broom sticks. The ends are cut so that it is the right length and then the wood is sanded until smooth.   For this recipe, a regular rolling pin will do just fine.

Make Ahead
Any unused dough can be wrapped in wax paper and then placed in freezer bags and frozen. Will keep in the freezer for 6 months. Simply thaw on counter for a few hours before using.

Uncooked spiral pies can be frozen for up to 6 months. Simply thaw on counter for a few hours before cooking.

food is love

3 greek sisters

PREPARED PHYLLO PIE TECHNIQUE

We know that you can't always prepare homemade phyllo. So in a pinch, use this prepared phyllo pie technique with our Chicken & Leek Filling, Kreatopita, and Leek Pie recipes instead.

1. Melt the butter in a small saucepan over low heat. Remove from the heat and skim away any foam. Use only the clarified butter and avoid the white milk solids that have settled on the bottom of the pan.

2. Gather two of the phyllo sheets and cover the remaining sheets with a damp cloth to avoid drying out. Lay the two sheets of phyllo along the bottom of a 9-x13-inch (33x23 cm) shallow baking dish. Allow the sheets to overlap in the center of the pan and the excess to hang over the sides of the pan. Brush the sheets lightly with some of the melted butter. Arrange another six sheets of phyllo in the same manner, brushing each sheet with melted butter. Add the filling of your choice and spread it evenly in the pan.

3. Gather the excess phyllo pastry hanging over the sides of the pan and fold over to enclose the filling. Brush each layer with melted butter. Lay the remaining two layers of phyllo pastry on the very top and allow the phyllo to wrinkle and fold to create a ruffled top. Brush with melted butter. Cover in plastic wrap and refrigerate for 30 minutes.

4. Remove from the refrigerator and lightly sprinkle the top of the pastry with water. Place in the middle of a preheated oven and bake until golden brown and crispy, about 45 minutes. Cut into serving pieces and serve warm or cold.

Ingredients
½ cup unsalted butter
10 sheets prepared phyllo pastry, thawed
1 Filling Recipe, cooled, page 119, 124 or 159.

Phyllo Pastry Tips
Always defrost phyllo pastry in the refrigerator overnight.

Any phyllo that you are not working with should be covered with a damp cloth to avoid drying out.

Rips or tears can easily be mended by brushing the sheet with butter and patching it up with another piece of phyllo.

Do not refreeze phyllo sheets once thawed as they will be difficult to work with for a second time. The phyllo will crack and crumble and will not fold properly.

Make Ahead
Prepared Phyllo pies can be frozen for up to 3 months. Simply thaw or cook from frozen.

Bake (350°F / 180°C)   Serves (6-8)   Time to Table (1 ½ hours)

food is love

Tasteful Tip

Before running the sausage meat through the hog casings, you can test it for proper seasonings by heating some olive oil in a frying pan over medium-low heat. Place a small piece of the ground sausage meat in the pan and cook until browned and cooked through. Taste. If you are not satisfied with the taste, adjust the seasonings and repeat until you are satisfied.

3 greek sisters

HOMEMADE ORANGE FENNEL SAUSAGES

Lokanika (loh-KAH-nee-kah)

Sausage making is a lost art that is slowly gaining traction. More and more people are looking to make their own. It is nice to know and be able to control what goes into the sausages you serve your family. Our recipe highlights sausage from the Peloponnese region with its pronounced and unique orange flavour. To prepare this recipe you will need a meat grinder and sausage stuffer.

Ingredients
5 lb (2½ kg) pork shoulder
(about 4:1 ratio of meat:fat)
15 ft hog casings
2 tbsp salt
2 tbsp dried oregano
Rind of 2 oranges, chopped
1 tbsp ground pepper
2 tsp sweet paprika
1½ tsp fennel seeds
1 tsp ground all spice
1 cup Ouzo

1. Begin by placing the meat, and a large bowl in the freezer for 2 hours. The process of grinding the meat will be much easier if the meat is chilled before beginning.

2. Meanwhile, place the hog casings in warm water for 30 minutes. Drain and cover in fresh water. Set aside until ready to use.

3. Remove the meat from the freezer and place on a cutting board. Use a sharp knife to cut the pork shoulder into smaller pieces. Do not trim away the fat. Run the meat and fat through the coarse die of a meat grinder and let the meat fall in a cold, large bowl.

4. Add the remaining ingredients to the bowl and mix the ingredients thoroughly using your hands. The mixture will feel a bit sticky. If desired, test the meat for proper seasonings. See tip on opposite page.

5. Place the bowl of sausage meat in the freezer for 30 minutes.

6. Check to see if there are any holes in your hog casings by running warm water through them. Discard any casings with holes.

7. Slip a casing onto the stuffing tube. Leave about 6-inches (15 cm) of casing off the end of the tube so that you can tie it off later.

8. Remove the meat from the freezer. Working in batches, crank the machine and push the meat down until it comes out of the stuffing tube and into the casing. Air will emerge first and meat will follow. Continue cranking and pushing meat down until all of the meat has been pushed through and into the casings. Ensure that some of the casing is left empty at the end and tie it off in a double knot. *Continued on next page.*

Recipe
Use this Homemade Sausage recipe to make our Spetzofai recipe on page 129.

food is love

Makes (15-20) Time to Table (5 hours) Diet (gf)

Homemade Orange Fennel Sausage recipe continued from previous page.

9   Using both hands, twist the sausage into 6-inch (15 cm) links by pinching the sausage and spinning it. Continue pinching the sausage in 6-inch (15 cm) increments. Spin the sausage in the opposite direction each time. Ensure that the links are tight and air bubbles are avoided. At the end of the coil tie it off in a double knot.

10 Let the sausages dry on a rack for at least two hours, ensuring as best as you can that they do not touch. Pierce any air bubbles with a needle. Store the sausages in the freezer until you are ready to cook them.

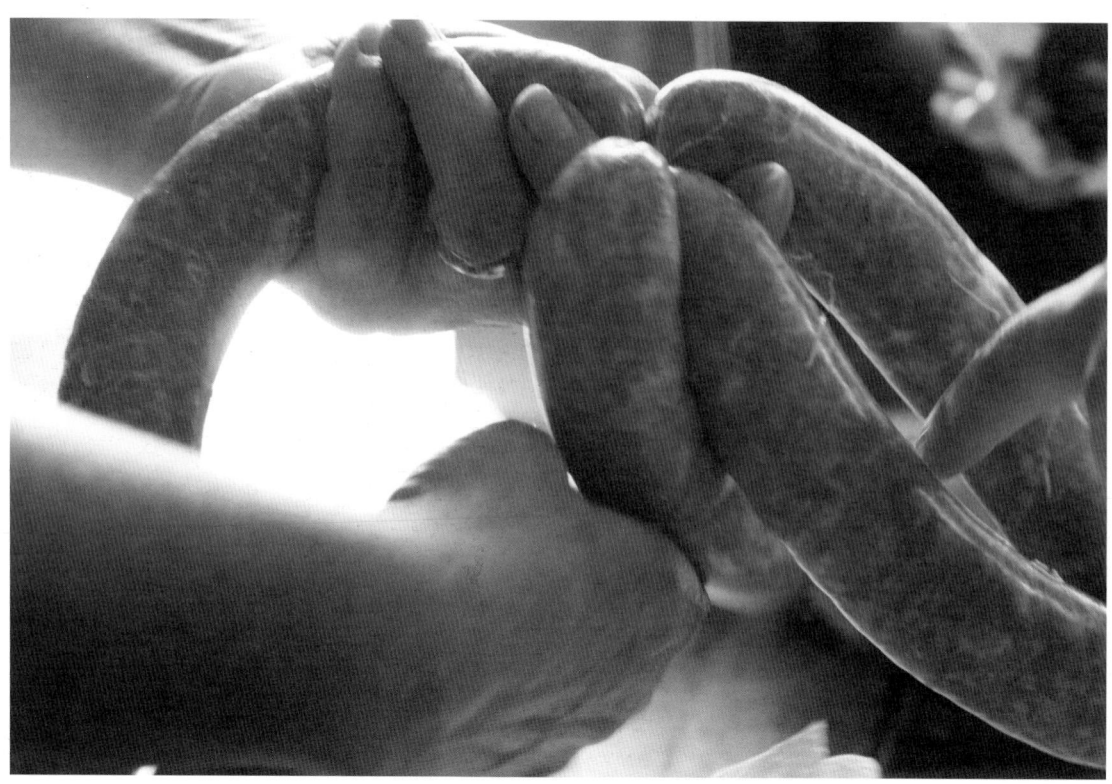

food is love

KOLIVA

(KOH-lee-vah)

Wheat berries are used to prepare Koliva, a memorial food that is prepared by the family members of a loved one who has passed away. Ladies will gather together and make a dish of boiled wheat berries that are then sweetened with sugar. Once cooked, the berries are pressed into tins or pie plates and dressed with almonds, raisins, pomegranate seeds and Confectioner's sugar. Silver candies or dragées also decorate the finished dish with elaborate crosses and repeating patterns. Often time, the initials of the deceased are also included. These plates are brought to the altar 3 days after a loved one has passed to receive a blessing. Following the liturgy the Koliva is then shared with all present. The ritual is repeated on the 9th day, the 40th day, 6 months and on the 1 year anniversary of the loved one's death. Recipes vary widely although all recipes use wheat berries to symbolize resurrection. We wanted to include our recipe here so that this tradition will not be lost, but carried on even when our elders are no longer here to guide us.

Ingredients

4 cups wheat berry
2 cups Sultana raisins
1 cup almonds, blanched & sliced
1 cup walnuts, chopped
1 cup sesame seeds, toasted
2 tsp coriander seeds, toasted and crushed
2 tsp ground cinnamon
1 tsp ground cloves
Breadcrumbs or almonds, finely ground
Confectioner's sugar
Almond confetti
Almonds, blanched, sliced
Silver dragées

1. Spread the wheat berry on a flat surface and check for small stones. Discard stones. Add the wheat berry to a pot of boiling water and boil for 15 minutes. Drain and replace with 5 cups water. Bring to a boil and continue boiling for 45 minutes. Remove the pot from the heat and set aside, covered for one hour.

2. Drain the wheat berry and rinse under cold water. To remove the excess water, lay the berry on a clean kitchen towel and set aside for 10 minutes.

3. Add the wheat berry to a large bowl along with the raisins, almonds, walnuts, sesame seeds, coriander seeds, cinnamon and cloves.

4. Mix and transfer the wheat berry mixture to a pie plate or platter and use your hands to firmly pat down the berries into the shape of a mound. Top the berry with enough breadcrumb to create a ½-inch (12 mm) layer. (The breadcrumb layer acts to protect the top layer of Confectioner's sugar from absorbing any excess water and thus discolouring.)

5. Use your hands or a piece of wax paper to firmly pat down the breadcrumb layer until smooth.

6. Using a fine sieve, add a ½-inch (12 mm) layer of Confectioner's sugar. Use your hands or a piece of wax paper to firmly pat down the Confectioner's sugar layer until smooth. *Continued on following page.*

3 greek sisters

Serves (20-30) Time to Table (3 ½ hours) Diet (v)

7   The Koliva is now ready to be decorated with almond confetti, sliced almonds, and dragées. Traditionally, crosses, flowers and initials of the deceased are added to the Koliva using almonds and dragées.

8   After the church service, the Koliva is tossed together in a large bowl so that the icing sugar is mixed thoroughly. The Koliva is divided into small cups and shared with everyone in your gathering.

food is love

3 greek sisters

food is love

Traditional Magheritsa

Traditional Magheritsa includes the use of organ meat. The recipe provided can easily incorporate these very traditional ingredients. Simply take the organ meat (liver, kidney, lung or heart) and cut them into bite-sized pieces. Place in a large pot and cover with water. Bring to a boil for 5 minutes and remove any foam. The organs can then be used in combination with the lamb, as we have suggested, or simply on their own with greens and Avgolemono sauce.

3 greek sisters

MAGHERITSA

(Mah-yeh-REE-tsa)

On Easter Sunday a lamb is typically roasted on a spit, but on the eve of that event, a soup is traditionally made that utilizes the lambs' organ meat; Magheritsa. Magheritsa is a traditional Easter soup eaten after a late night church service on the eve of Easter Sunday; It is the first taste of meat that those practrising Lent will have eaten in 40 days. Back when families raised their own lambs, and wasted very little, they didn't hesitate to eat organ meat. Nowadays, eating organ meat can raise some valid concerns and people are timid at the thought of eating meats like liver, tripe, and heart. Because we love tradition, and because Magheritsa is actually delicious, we have modified the original recipe to include bits of lamb meat in a creamy broth, lots of dill, and a few onions and greens. This modern Magheritsa recipe is a wonderful way to continue the tradition of eating Magheritsa on the Eve of Easter Sunday, without the inevitable squeamish dinner guest going hungry.

1. Liberally salt and pepper the loin chops on both sides. Heat the olive oil in a large saucepan over high heat. Brown the chops, about 3-4 minutes per side. Reduce the heat to medium and add the shallots and sauté for 2 minutes. Add the garlic and sauté for a minute further.

2. Add the wine, increase the heat to high and bring to a boil. Let the wine reduce by half. Add the scallions and dill and stir. Add the water and salt, and bring to a boil. Reduce the heat to medium-low and low-boil, covered, for 1 hour.

3. Add the lettuce, stir, and continue cooking, covered, for 30 minutes.

4. Remove the meat from the pot, it should be falling off the bone. Cut the meat into smaller bite-sized pieces and return it to the pot.

5. For the Avgolemono sauce, carefully remove 1 cup of the hot cooking liquid from the pot. Stir in the lemon juice and set aside. Add the egg whites to the bowl of a stand-mixer fitted with a whisk attachment. Beat the whites on high-speed until soft peaks form. With the mixer running add the egg yolks and slowly add the cup of hot liquid and lemon juice. Ensure that the liquid is added slowly so that the eggs do not curdle. Adding hot liquid slowly to eggs is referred to as tempering.

6. Return the Avgolemono sauce to the pot. Hold the pot with both hands and slowly tilt it back and forth. Serve.

Ingredients
1 lb (500 g) lamb loin chops
Salt & Pepper
2 tbsp olive oil
2 shallots, minced
3 garlic cloves, roughly chopped
1 cup white wine
5 scallions, chopped, white & pale green parts
1 cup fresh dill, chopped
4 cups water
1 tsp salt
2 cups red leaf lettuce, chopped

For the Avgolemono
1 cup cooking liquid
Juice of 1½ lemons
2 eggs, separated

Substitution
Bone-in lamb blade shoulder chops or lamb shanks can be used.

food is love

Serves 4   Time to Table 2 hours   Diet gf

GLOSSARY OF TERMS

Bulgur Wheat
Wheat that has been soaked, cooked, and dried before the bran is removed. Used often in salads and side dishes.

Dragée
A dragée is a bite-sized form of confectionary. They are colourful with a hard outer shell. Used for decoration when making Koliva.

Feta Cheese
See Glossary of Cheeses

Geranium Leaves
Scented geraniums, which Greeks call arbaroiza, are used to prepare many spoon sweets. We like to use it when making the grape and quince spoon sweet. Scented geraniums, rose, lemon and mint, can easily be found in garden nurseries. They make wonderful additions to garden pots. Geranium leaves are added to spoon sweets infusing them with their scent. The leaves are then discarded before serving. Scented geraniums can also be referred to as the Mosquito plant, as the scent the leaves give off is said to repel mosquitoes.

Greek Extra Virgin Olive Oil
A 100% natural cold pressed olive oil. The olive oil comes from the first pressing of the olives without any chemicals or hot water added. Make sure to check the label on the oil containers to ensure that the oil is a product of Greece. Olive oil should be stored in a cool, dry place. Olive oil does not get better with age, it should be consumed within one year of production.

Halloumi
See Glossary of Cheeses

Hilopites
Egg noodles are popular throughout Greece. They can be made into long noodles, or cut into square shapes. They are often added to braised dishes.

Koliva
Koliva is a memorial food made by the relatives of the deceased. It consists of wheat berries, almonds, raisins and Confectioner's sugar. The mixture is presented in large tins and elaborately decorated with silver candies or dragées. Koliva is brought to the church and shared with those who have come to pay their respects.

Manouri
See Glossary of Cheeses

Mastiha
Originally used as a chewing gum, mastiha is the sap found on trees that grow on the island of Chios. Only the trees on this island release this sap, often referred to as "tears". Mastiha or mastic comes in the form of resinous granules but can sometimes be ground into powder.

Mavrodaphne
A very sweet red dessert wine. Originating in Peloponnese, Greece, this wine has a nice fruity flavour. Mavrodaphne substitutions: Madeira, Banyuls, or other sweet dessert wine.

Metaxa Brandy
A Greek distilled spirit, it is essentially a blend of brandy and wine. It comes in 5 varieties: Three Stars, Five Stars, Seven Stars, Twelve Stars and the Grand Reserve.

Ouzo
A strong alcohol that is heavily flavoured with anise. Other flavourings come from spices such as cardamom, star anise seed, coriander and lime flowers. Every region of Greece creates their own version of Ouzo. A good bottle of Ouzo can be found at your local liquor store.

Saganaki
Literally means "little frying pan" but today the term is synonymous with a popular appetizer that consists of fried salty cheeses.

Saffron
Saffron is cultivated in Krokos, Macedonia from the Crocus plant, for two weeks in the autumn. It is a labour intensive process making saffron very expensive. Saffron is used in cooking to enhance flavour and colour, but Greeks do not cook with it often. It is mostly an exported product.

Sausage Casing
Sausage casing is the material used to encase the filling of sausages. There are both natural and artificial casings. Natural hog casings come from the intestine of the pig. Artificial are made from collagen, or cellulose. Natural casings are edible and also allow for smoking of sausages. Some artificial casings are not edible and need to be removed after cooking.

Semolina
Semolina is made from hard durum wheat. It can be found coarsely ground or finely ground into flour.

Spelt
Spelt or hulled wheat is an ancient nutritious grain with a nutty flavour. It can be used in the same way as wheat to make breads and pasta.

Spoon Sweets
Spoons sweets have a long-standing tradition in Greek culture. It is a way of preserving the bountiful fruit found throughout the country. Fruit such as cherries, grapes, and quince are sweetened with sugar. Some fruit is further flavoured with rose petals, or geranium leaves and served on small demitasse spoons

Wheat Berries
Wheat berries are whole kernels of wheat used to make Koliva.

HERBS

Herbs add not only colour to a dish, but flavour and health benefits. In Greece, herbs are gathered from the gardens and the hillsides. Every balcony has pots filled with basil, the king of all herbs. Below is a list of common herbs found in everyday cooking.

All of the herbs listed below are added fresh to dishes, except for oregano. It is the one herb that is most often used dried. Oregano imparts more flavour to meals when dried. Oregano is gathered from the hills, tied into bundles and left to dry in the hot sun. These bundles of oregano are kept throughout the year and used almost daily.

Anise - Glykaniso (Glee-KAH-nee-soh)
Basil - Vasilikos (Vah-see-lee-KOS)
Bay leaf - Dafni (THA-fnee)
Chamomile - Hamomili (Hah-moh-MEE-lee)
Dill - Anithos (AH-nee-thos)
Fennel - Maratho (MAH-rah-tho)
Marjoram - Mantzourana (Mah-TZOU-rah-nah)
Mint - Diosmos (Dee-OH-smos)
Oregano - Rigani (REE-gah-nee)
Parsley - Maidanos (Mah-ee-tha-NOS)
Rosemary - Dendrolivano (Then-droh-LEE-vah-noh)
Sage - Faskomilo (Fah-SKOH-mee-loh)
Thyme - Thymari (Thee-MAH-ree)

3 greek sisters

Drying oregano is something we enjoy doing when we visit Greece as the hillsides are covered with this fragrant herb. Drying oregano is simple to do and does not require any fancy equipment. Simply cut the oregano plant at the base and tie it into small bundles with twine, elastic bands or twist ties. Hang them upside down outside in the hot sun until the oregano becomes dry. The length of time depends on the weather. If it is very hot and sunny, then it may be dry in as little as 2-3 days. If your days are wreaked with humid weather, then the oregano will mold before it ever dries. You need the hot summer sun to smile down on the fragrant bundles. If the weather does not seem to work in your favour then simply move the drying process to the indoors.

An oven can be used to dry herbs. Spread the oregano on baking sheets lined with parchment paper, and set your oven to the lowest temperature. The heat from the oven will also be able to dry the herb. Keep a close eye so that it does not burn.

Once dry, the dried oregano needs to be removed from the stalks. If your hands have been toughened over the years, then you can simply rub the woody stalks between your hands. This back and forth motion removes the dried leaves from the stalks. The fragrance that is released during this stage is intoxicating.

Dried oregano will last for months. Always rub the dried leaves between your fingers when adding to meals to release all the fragrant oils.

food is love

GLOSSARY OF CHEESES

Goats can be seen grazing the hillsides of Greece, sheep can be seen passing through villages on early morning walks. The milk from goats and sheep has played a significant role in Greek kitchens. Milk has always been a valuable commodity to Greek families, and so it was important that no part of the milk was wasted. You will find that Greeks even use the whey to make several delicious cheeses. Greeks consume a lot of cheese. It finds its way to the table at every meal.

Anthotiro
A cheese that has been made for centuries using sheep's and goat's milk. It is essentially a variation of Mizithra. The name means "Flower cheese". It is smooth, hard and moist with a fine, crumbly texture.

Feta
Feta is the most commonly known Greek cheese in North America. Made from sheep's milk, it literally means "a slice". The shape of feta reflects the container that was used to make the cheese, whether it is a pottery bowl, wooden barrel or a woven basket. Feta has been made by nomadic shepherds for centuries. It is a salty cheese and needs to be kept in brine. Although some make feta with cow's milk, the taste is inferior and is not authentic feta cheese.

Graviera
A cheese from Dodoni, Naxos and Crete. This is a hard table cheese, but mild in flavour. After feta, this is the most popular of the Greek cheeses. It is much like a Gruyere or Swiss cheese, it is both sweet and fruity, it has tiny holes and a rich creamy feel.

Halloumi
Made in Cyprus, it is the perfect grilling/frying cheese as it can withstand high temperatures. It is a semi-hard unripened cheese made from sheep's and goat's milk.

Kaseri
Kaseri is made with a combination of sheep's and goat's milk. There is no rind. It is smooth, creamy, springy and light yellow in colour. It is a wonderful table cheese, and can be used for melting, grilling or for baking recipes. It resembles the Italian Provolone cheese.

Kefalotiri
Made from sheep's milk, this is a delicious table cheese. It is also used for recipes that call for grated cheeses. This cheese has a sharp finish.

Kefalograviera
A salty hard cheese used for "saganaki" dishes made popular by every Greek restaurant in North America. This cheese is lightly floured, fried and flambéed. It is dramatically extinguished with lemon juice.

Manouri
A soft, creamy, white cheese that is both rind less and salt less. This cheese originates in Crete and Macedonia with a texture reminiscent of a cream cheese.

Metsovone
A smoked cheese made with cow's milk and the addition of sheep's or goat's milk.

Mizithra
Mizithra is a wonderful grating cheese. It is often used in pastries or with various pasta dishes. It is a semi-hard cheese that comes in the shape of a large ball.

Xynotyro
The name of this cheese literally means "sour cheese", but in fact it is a hard, flaky cheese, that melts in your mouth. It has a distinct sweet and sour flavour.

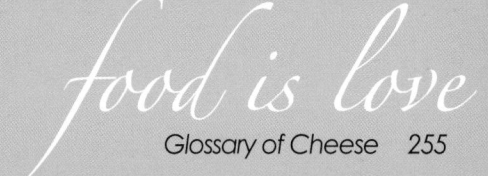

food is love

INDEX

INDEX *continued*

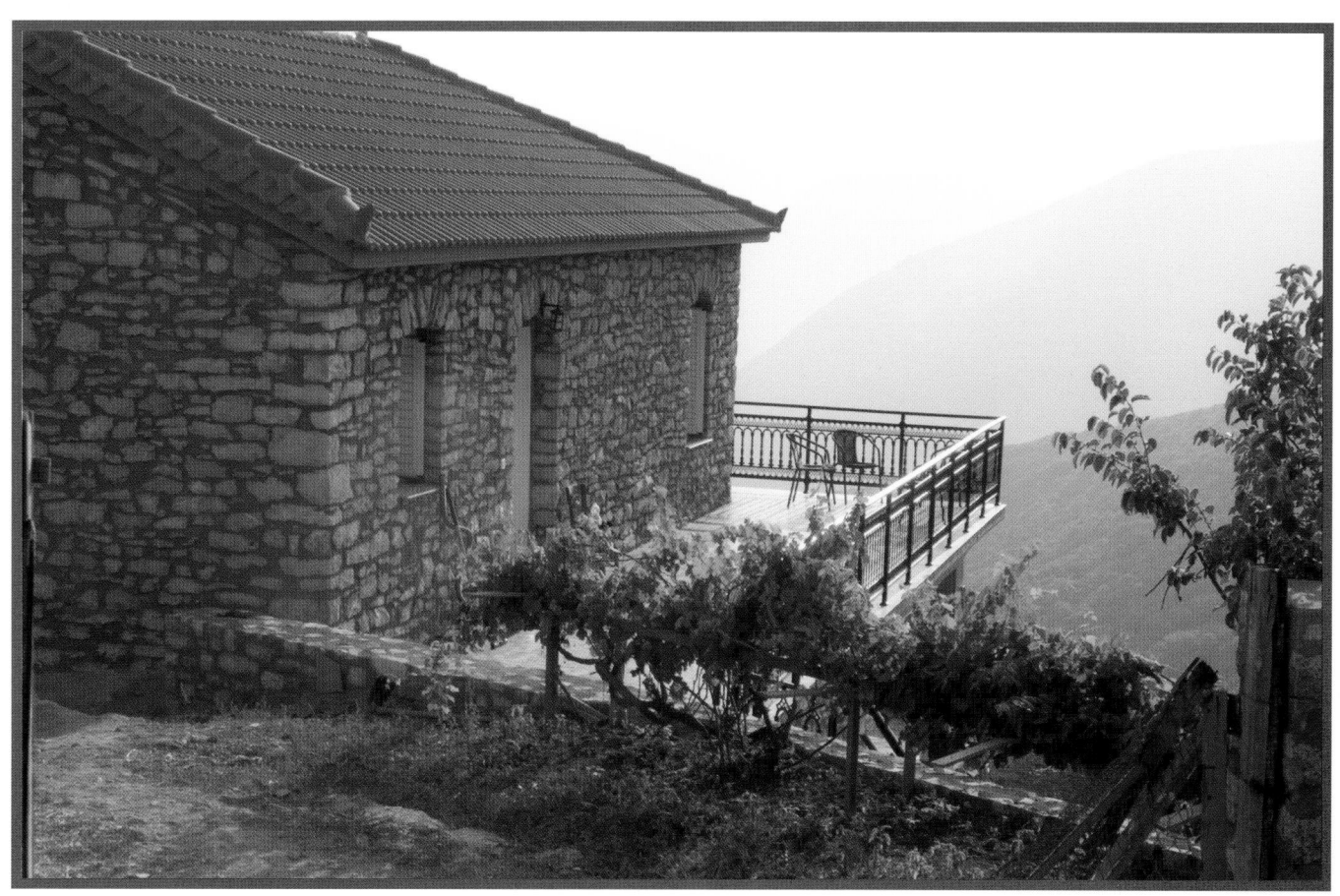

The House
2012

Thank you

Thank you to all the fans that supported us with our first book. Your support gave us the courage and incentive to write a second one.

Thank you to iPhone - for keeping our brains and thoughts connected 24 hours a day.

Thank you once again to Georges Philippouci for overseeing the printing of our book. We could not do it without you.

This past year we had the good fortune of meeting ladies who have mastered the art of phyllo-making. Eleni Souglis and Eleni Koumbridis, along with Eleni Orfanidis graciously shared their secrets to making flaky homemade phyllo with us for this book. Thank you.

We also want to thank Christine Kolinas and Betty Vasilopoulou for their help in sharing both recipes and stories with us, not only for this book, but over the years. Both of you will always be dear to our hearts. Remembering all the love we shared in that red brick house in Toronto many years ago still brings tears to our eyes.

A special thank you to Theo Yianni and Thea Maria in Greece for assisting us in rebuilding our home, and for watching over it in our absence. Greece for us is more than the beauty of the mountains and the sea, it is family like you.

Thank you to Jonathan for sharing your beautiful family vacation photos.

To our husbands, Jonathan, Sean and Éric, you are the most supportive, loving people. You are always there for us and we thank you.

Thank you Mom and Dad

This book would not be possible without our mom and dad. Each and every morning begins with a phone call - a gentle reminder that they are there if we need them. And it seems that we always do. They are by our side when shopping for groceries, they are by our side when washing our dishes, they are by our side when testing recipes, they are by our side when writing stories, and they are by our side when we just need them to be by our side. We hope this book makes you proud.

Our Beginning - Georgios & Konstantina

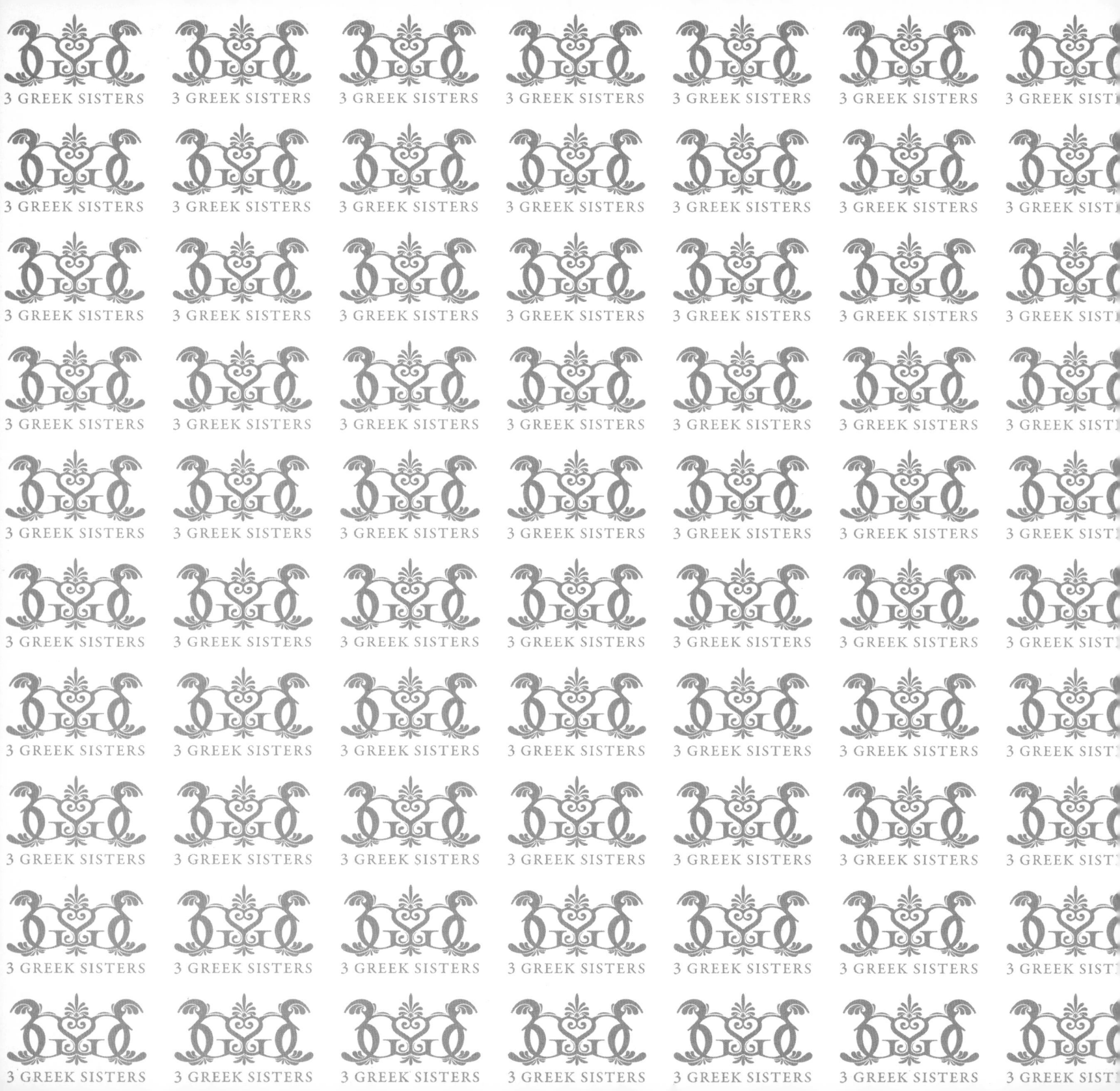

Printed for

01/13
Montréal, Québec Canada
First Printing